W9-BNY-357

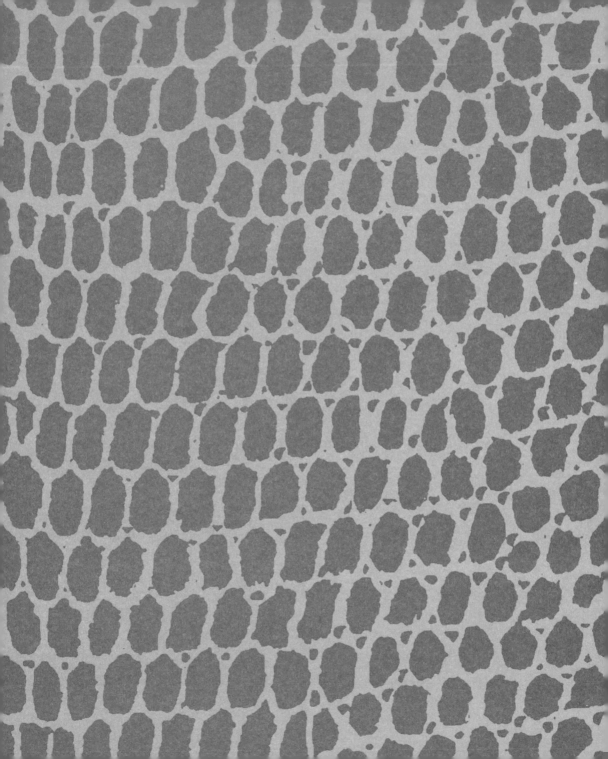

# Setup and
# Care of
# Saltwater
# Aquariums

**DAVID E. BORUCHOWITZ**

ANIMAL PLANET ♥ PET CARE LIBRARY

*Setup and Care of Saltwater Aquariums*

*Project Team*
Editor: Craig Sernotti
Copy Editor: Neal Pronek
Design Concept: Leah Lococo Ltd., Stephanie Krautheim
Design Layout: Mary Ann Kahn

*T.F.H. Publications*
President/CEO: Glen S. Axelrod
Executive Vice President: Mark E. Johnson
Publisher: Christopher T. Reggio
Production Manager: Kathy Bontz

*Discovery Communications, Inc. Book Development Team*
Marjorie Kaplan, President, Animal Planet Media
Carol LeBlanc, Vice President, Licensing
Elizabeth Bakacs, Vice President, Creative Services
Brigid Ferraro, Director, Licensing
Peggy Ang, Vice President, Animal Planet Marketing
Caitlin Erb, Licencing Specialist

T.F.H. Publications, Inc.
One TFH Plaza
Third and Union Avenues
Neptune City, NJ 07753

Exterior design ©2007 Discovery Communications, Inc. Animal Planet, logo and Animusings are trademarks of Discovery Communications, Inc., used under license. All rights reserved. *animalplanet.com*

Interior design, text, and photos ©2007 T.F.H. Publications, Inc.

All rights reserved. No part of this publication may be reproduced, stored, or transmitted in any form, or by any means electronic, mechanical or otherwise, without written permission from T.F.H. Publications, except where permitted by law. Requests for permission or further information should be directed to the above address.

Printed and bound in China
08 09 10 11 12   3 5 7 9 8 6 4 2

Library of Congress Cataloging-in-Publication Data
Boruchowitz, David E.
  Setup and care of saltwater aquariums / David E. Boruchowitz.
    p. cm. – (Animal Planet pet care library)
  Includes index.
  ISBN 978-0-7938-3789-2 (alk. paper)
  1. Marine aquariums. I. Animal Planet (Television network) II. Title.
  SF457.1.B667 2007
  639.34'2–dc22
                            2007010384

This book has been published with the intent to provide accurate and authoritative information in regard to the subject matter within. While every reasonable precaution has been taken in preparation of this book, the author and publisher expressly disclaim responsibility for any errors, omissions, or adverse effects arising from the use or application of the information contained herein. The techniques and suggestions are used at the reader's discretion and are not to be considered a substitute for veterinary care. If you suspect a medical problem consult your veterinarian.

*The Leader In Responsible Animal Care For Over 50 Years!®*
www.tfh.com

CENTRAL
*Garden & Pet*

# Table of Contents

# Introduction

A transcontinental 18-wheeler sits by the curb in front of your house. You sit behind the wheel. The keys are in your hand. On the floor are three pedals: clutch, brake, throttle. On your right are the controls for the multiple-ratio drive-axle transmission: split switches and gearshift. A handwritten sign above them says, "Remember, floating is better than double clutching." Okay, drive to town!

**U**nless you are a commercial truck driver, it is unlikely you will be able to get the rig moving, even if you are accomplished at driving a manual-transmission four-wheel-drive SUV. If all you've ever driven are automatic-transmission cars, you have no chance. If by some miracle you did get the vehicle going down the road, you would almost certainly fail to negotiate the first turn you encounter.

And yet, commercial trucking companies do not require their drivers to have PhDs—driving big rigs isn't rocket science. While many truckers are big, burly men, many are not, and there are even petite women in their ranks—driving big rigs doesn't require great brute strength. And there is no emphasis on ballet or gymnastics training in truck driving schools—driving semis is not a matter of grace or form.

Still, a few hours in trucker training would convince you that professional drivers are masters of a very complicated system of control, one that requires specific knowledge, mastery of various physical tasks, and precise coordination of movements in exact sequence. As with many other jobs in our society, this is a skill that requires training and education and will improve with practice.

Successfully maintaining a marine aquarium is similar. There is certain knowledge you must have, certain equipment required, and experience or

*The harlequin tuskfish* Choerodon fasciatus *is a beautiful, hardy, and peaceful wrasse, but it gets too large (up to a foot/30 cm) for our protocol. Buying this fish would be the kind of mistake that drives many people away from the hobby when their fish die. The advice in this book will help save you from that disappointment.*

practice needed for improvement. It isn't all that difficult to learn, but without the appropriate training, you don't stand a chance.

Think of this book as your training manual. It contains what you need to know, it describes what you need to buy, and it will warn you of the common pitfalls that cause so many new aquarists to fail and give up in despair.

Does it contain everything there is to know about marine aquariums? Hardly. Is the advice here the only advice that will work? Certainly not. But the path outlined here will bring you success, and once you have a successful marine aquarium, you can, if you want, go on to learn more and to try more challenging setups. Be aware that there are many paths that will bring you to a successful marine aquarium, and there is a lot of advice out there. Some is unnecessarily complicated, as marine aquarists tend to be very interested in chemistry and biochemistry; you do need to know some science to succeed as a marine aquarist, but not all that much. Many beginners' guides fail to keep things simple because they try to cover everything; you don't need to know everything to get started. A few books even give bad advice, perpetuating old myths that have not stood the test of time; obviously following such advice is not a good idea. Keep in mind that we are intentionally not telling you about a lot of things; someone you speak to might insist that you understand a certain topic; well, it might be one of the ones we've chosen to avoid. Just trust us. If we think you absolutely have to know something to succeed, we'll cover it. Otherwise, it can wait.

What we've done in this book is distill a huge accumulation of experience, mingled with sound science, to produce a protocol that will enable you to succeed with your first marine aquarium. This necessitates that we make a lot of choices for you, and some admittedly will be somewhat arbitrary. But the alternative is for you to be inundated with an impossible barrage of choices that need to be made, some critical—only you will have no basis on which to make them or even to know which are critical and which are not!

So here's a promise: follow the advice in this book, ignoring what other well-intentioned people try to tell you, until you have a saltwater aquarium up and running for at least six months, and you will succeed. At that point, this book will have served its purpose, and you can start delving into the enormous body of knowledge and literature about the marine aquarium hobby, following whatever paths interest you.

## A Note Before Continuing

This book is intended as a reference, not as a map. In other words, it assumes that you will read it entirely before buying the first piece of equipment and that you will follow the protocol exactly in setting up your aquarium. As just one example of why this is so important, the discussion of setting up the tank and stocking it follows logically after our discussion of the things you need to know and those you need to have, but several of the steps in setting up an aquarium require knowledge from the later chapter on fish health. So read the book all the way through at least once, and only then go back and start at the beginning, prepared to follow the steps.

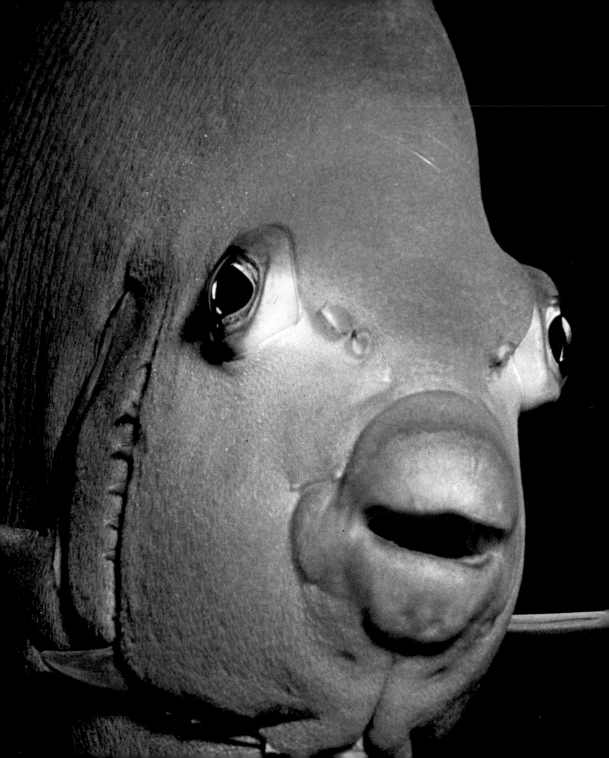

# Chapter 1

## Why Do YOU

# Want a Saltwater Aquarium?

What are you looking for in considering a marine aquarium for your home or workplace? There are many reasons people choose to set up a saltwater fish tank.

## Beauty & Relaxation

People usually cannot walk past a marine aquarium without stopping to *ooh* and *ah* at the fish. The colors, shapes, and behaviors of coral reef fishes are diverse and exotic. Some of them look like they sport neon paint, and the bizarre shapes look like something out of someone's fantasy. Their colors are so extreme that many look as if they were blank fish outlines that children were allowed to color in—half one color, half another, stripes and polka dots together, etc. Reef tanks go a step further and also house fascinating invertebrates—the corals, anemones, clams, and other colorful creatures that in many ways seem more like plants than animals.

Besides being a thing of exquisite beauty, a marine aquarium captures your interest, soothes your nerves, and draws you into another world. When a marine tank is situated in a doctor's waiting room or an airport lounge, people often are reluctant to break away when they are called or when their flight is announced. For many people, this is what they want when they decide to set up a saltwater tank in their home or office—something that will add beauty and bring a bit of nature into their lives while providing a relaxing scene to watch.

## Love of the Ocean

Some people become marine aquarists because they are enthralled by the ocean in its immensity and diversity, and they want to bring a little of that into their homes. Childhood summers at the beach, scuba diving experience, time spent at sea, or even just dedicated attention to television documentaries—

*Some marine fish will amaze you with their breathtaking coloration.*

## Participation

Children of all ages are fascinated by a marine aquarium. Depending on their age, they can participate by handing you things, helping with chores, or even doing some maintenance by themselves, with supervision. Just make sure the task matches their maturity and abilities.

whatever originally caught their interest—these lovers of the sea find that a saltwater aquarium brings back the sensations, the memories.

Others come to the marine hobby through an interest in conservation. That might surprise you, since you may have heard accusations against the aquarium hobby as exploitive and damaging to our natural coral reefs. While harvesting livestock from the ocean can contribute to the overall destruction of a reef, the portion that can be credited in any way to the aquarium hobby is minuscule compared to that from harvesting for human consumption, tourism, pollution, and coastline development and urbanization. In fact, the effects of agricultural runoff and silting from construction projects are the largest threat reefs face.

Far from being destructive, in fact, the aquarium hobby serves to preserve our reefs in three major ways:

- *Through education and raising awareness.* People work to save the things they love, and they can love only the things they know. The marine aquarium hobby brings the tropical coral reefs to people who would otherwise never experience these exquisite natural resources.
- *By direct involvement in conservation efforts.* Hobbyists have been the driving force in creating sustainable fisheries, both in terms of the fish populations and in terms of empowering the local people to make a meaningful living from the ornamental fish industry.
- *From captive breeding programs.* Aquarists have led the development of successful protocols for breeding many marine species. Captive breeding provides two protections for the natural reef: it lightens the fishing pressure, and it provides captive stock, which is highly preferable for aquarium stocking— and which is much better than nothing if the worst happens and a species goes extinct in the wild.

### Stepping Up

Then again, you might already be an aquarist who has enjoyed maintaining one or more freshwater aquaria. Maybe you've even bred various species of freshwater fish. Now marine fish have

*If you have already mastered freshwater aquarium husbandry, you will find that many of your skills will carry over to a marine aquarium.*

caught your eye, or perhaps you're looking for a new challenge and see salt water as the next stage in your hobby. You certainly do not have to master freshwater aquarium keeping in order to succeed with a saltwater system, but there is certainly a degree of transference involved, and the skills a freshwater aquarist has mastered will serve well during a foray into the salty side. What did it for me many years ago was walking into my favorite fish store and seeing damselfish on sale for less money than the cichlids I had gone in to purchase.

## What Type of Setup?

There are many types of saltwater aquaria. The most common are:

- FO: Fish-only tanks contain nothing but fish and non-living substrate and decorations.

- FOWLR: Fish-only-with-live-rock tanks add the beauty and natural filtration provided by live rock, which we will discuss in Chapter 3.
- (Mini) Reef: Reef tanks contain a reef made of live rock and populated with various sessile invertebrates—corals, anemones, clams, gorgonians, tube worms, etc. A reef tank calls for very expensive high output lighting systems, since many of these invertebrates are photosynthetic. Very few fish (sometimes none) are stocked, to keep the nutrient level low.

Our protocol, although it calls for live rock, can be used for a FO setup. Extra care would have to be paid to water quality, since the filtration benefits of the rock would be absent, and the aquarium would appear rather sterile in comparison to a FOWLR setup. That, however, is a choice you can make and still stay within the protocol. A reef system, though, is outside our protocol.

## Reef vs. Fish

While it is true that a reef tank focuses on invertebrates and contains fish secondarily, there are also philosophical differences between a modern reef tank and a regular marine aquarium. The reef aquarist concentrates on *control*. The name of the game is to maintain a tight control on the precise water chemistry in the aquarium. Dedicated reefers take pride

in keeping calcium concentrations, alkalinity, redox potential, trace element levels, and a host of other water parameters within strict bounds. They make use of equipment like calcium reactors, refractometers, redox meters, dosing pumps, and even computerized controllers.

The result of all this attention to chemistry is typically a drop-dead gorgeous system worthy of the pride its owner takes in it. This does not mean, however, that someone has to do all that to succeed with a marine tank, even one in which there is live rock and perhaps a few hardy invertebrates. That is the approach taken here. People do enter the hobby successfully at the reef level, but it is much more common for aquarists to succeed first with non-reef marine systems. There is no way to make setting up and maintaining a reef tank simple or easy—but there is for a FO or FOWLR system, namely the protocol established in these pages.

*The coral reef is a complex and fragile ecosystem. A marine aquarium can serve to increase people's awareness of conservation issues regarding tropical reefs.*

# Chapter 2

# What You

# Need to Know

It makes sense to talk about the little science you need to know before we look at the equipment you are going to need so that you can understand why you need it. If science isn't your strong suit, don't worry. If you've ever read about marine aquarium chemistry or talked to aquarists about it, especially don't worry! This will be practically painless, I promise. You simply have to agree not to want explanations. Believe me, once you get one successful marine aquarium up and running, you'll have plenty of time to delve into all the intricacies of marine chemistry—if you want to. For now, just learn what you need to achieve that first success.

## Properties of Water

Not surprisingly, the physical and chemical properties of water are centrally important in any aquarium. Because ocean water is a complex mixture of hundreds of dissolved substances, the physical and chemical properties of water are even more important in the marine aquarium. Keeping the water within certain parameters is the key to success. That is why you cannot escape a little bit of chemistry.

## Salinity

Salinity refers to the amount of dissolved salts in a sample of water. Any and all salts contribute to a sample's salinity. In seawater the greatest salt concentration is of sodium chloride, table salt, but there are dozens of other salts as well. Salts of calcium and magnesium are especially significant. In fact, the exact composition of seawater is extremely complex and includes almost all of the elements that exist. If you wanted to mix up some water for your aquarium from scratch, you would need to know a very great deal about the chemistry of seawater. Fortunately, aquarium salt mix manufacturers have gone to great effort and expense to research and to produce quality products that will create an excellent substitute for natural ocean water.

Salinity can be measured in various ways, but for your purposes with your first saltwater aquarium, a measurement of specific gravity, which is closely related to salinity, will suffice. When salts dissolve into water, the weight of a specific volume of the water increases compared to the same volume of absolutely pure water; at a given temperature, the more solids that dissolve into the water, the more the solution weighs. At aquarium temperatures the water should have a specific gravity of about 1.025.

Saltwater Aquariums

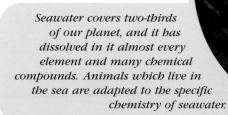

*Seawater covers two-thirds of our planet, and it has dissolved in it almost every element and many chemical compounds. Animals which live in the sea are adapted to the specific chemistry of seawater.*

## Why Not Natural?

If you live near the ocean, you might think that you can save a lot of trouble and expense by using natural seawater in your aquarium. Artificial seawater, however, is preferable. Aside from the fact that it is pretty much impossible to find unpolluted water anywhere near populated shores, ocean water is full of plankton—microscopic and tiny living organisms that can quickly die in an aquarium. They then begin to decompose, which seriously and negatively affects the water quality. Seawater can also introduce disease or parasites to your tank. Artificial seawater eliminates these concerns and is superior in another way as well: it is formulated to maintain correct water chemistry in an aquarium longer than natural seawater can.

Specific gravity is easily measured with a hydrometer. Our protocol calls for a swing-arm hydrometer, which consists of a narrow clear plastic case in which a plastic arrow swings. The case is filled with a water sample, and the arm swings up a certain distance, depending on the specific gravity of the sample. Along the arc (which is what the arm's tip describes as it pivots) are markings indicating the specific gravity readings. These devices are made for aquarium use and are calibrated for the correct temperature. We'll talk about mixing up water for your aquarium in a little while. For now just remember that you'll be testing it with the hydrometer and that you want the water to measure close to 1.025.

## pH

The strange abbreviation "pH" stands for a measurement of the amount of acid or base in a solution. You're probably familiar with common acids like vinegar, lemon juice, and battery acid and common bases like lye, baking soda, and ammonia. Acids and bases can be either weak or strong, which means they are either slightly or highly chemically active. For example, both concentrated battery acid and a concentrated lye solution will burn you if they make contact with your skin. Sometimes it is important to know just how strong or reactive an acidic or basic solution is. That's where pH comes in.

The pH scale is an inverse logarithmic measure of the relative activities of hydronium and hydroxide ions in a solution. (Don't worry—I just threw that in to show you what you're missing by following the protocol in this book rather than taking a more conventional route to aquarium keeping!) That definition is perfectly true, but it's also totally unnecessary for you to understand at this point in your career as an aquarist. In fact, many

*It is important to monitor your tank's pH level. Not having it within the correct range can be harmful to your fish.*

aquarists of all types spend way too much time worrying about pH. Here are two things you need to know:

1. The pH scale is centered on a neutral reading of 7.0. A higher reading indicates a basic solution, and a lower reading indicates an acidic solution. The table to the right lists some common substances and their typical pH values.
2. The pH of a marine aquarium should always be between 8.1 and 8.3. In fact, keeping it at a constant 8.3 is best.

That's all you really need to know about pH, except that you can test the pH of your water with a simple test kit. Just make sure the kit is designed for a saltwater aquarium, not a freshwater one.

You may be asking why you need to know about pH at all. Well, that's because it is very important to maintain a constant pH in your aquarium. To do that you have to understand a little bit about another chemical concept: alkalinity.

## Alkalinity

Although it is chemically complex, the concept of alkalinity is very easy to understand in terms of aquarium setup

| pH | |
| --- | --- |
| **Substance** | **pH** |
| Battery Acid | 0.5 |
| Stomach Acid | 1 |
| Cola or Vinegar | 2 to 3 |
| Orange Juice | 3 to 4 |
| Beer | 4.5 |
| Milk | 6.5 |
| Water, Chemically Pure | 7 |
| Human Blood | 7.4 |
| Toothpaste | 8 |
| Seawater | 8.3 |
| Hand Soaps | 9 to 10 |
| Ammonia (Household) | 11.5 |
| Lye (Household) | 13.5 |

and maintenance: the measurement of alkalinity reveals the ability of a sample of water to resist a change in pH when acids or bases are added. Various chemicals in natural sea water known as buffers can neutralize acids or bases, and artificial salt mixes have even more of these neutralizing chemicals.

This is important because the biological processes in an aquarium—fish metabolism, decomposition, waste degradation—all produce acids. That means that the pH can drop as time goes on. The drop in pH is in itself dangerous to your fish, but it also indicates that wastes are accumulating, which presents additional danger.

Water with high alkalinity will resist a drop in pH (which means a rise in the amount of acid) for longer than water with low alkalinity. Since artificial sea salt mixes contain special buffers, the water in your aquarium will have high alkalinity. That is good, but obviously at some point the buffers

can be used up, and when there are none left, the acid produced in the aquarium will begin to accumulate, and the pH of the water will drop. Do you add buffers to make up for this? No!

By the time the alkalinity of your aquarium water is exhausted, lots of other problems may have accumulated. In fact, *if* the pH drops in your tank, conditions are probably already bad, and you should work to avoid any change in pH. The purpose of this discussion has been to explain that it is important to maintain a pH of 8.3. Making regular partial water changes is the best way to keep up the alkalinity in your tank, since the new salt water will contain a fresh supply of buffers. A dropping pH is a very good indicator that you need to step up your water changes.

## Getting Rid of Wastes

Imagine that a puppy is placed into an aquarium that has a wire mesh top. There is a layer of wood shavings on the bottom. The puppy receives fresh water and food on a regular basis. How long until the tank becomes uninhabitable? This is not much different from the situation for fish in an aquarium. In fact, for them it is worse, since the puppy

*Fish have no choice but to breathe the same water in which their wastes dissolve. Their water, therefore, must constantly be cleaned and replaced.*

does not directly breathe in its own wastes, but fish are forced to breathe the same water into which their wastes dissolve. Make no mistake, fish wastes are toxic, and in sufficient concentration they will kill your fish.

There are four ways that fish wastes are properly managed in an aquarium:

1. Dilution. The water in an aquarium immediately dilutes any fish wastes. The amount of wastes that can dissolve into the water before they become appreciable and conditions begin to deteriorate depends on many factors, including the size of the aquarium, the size and number of fish, the amount of food fed, filtration, and water changes.

2. Filtration. Various types of filtration can remove waste products or convert them into less harmful substances. Most filters consist of a vessel with one or more filtration media through which aquarium water flows. There are several types of filtration, and any given filtering device can employ one or more of them. Of them all, biofiltration is by far the most important. Skimming is an adjunct to filtration, and it is an important part of waste management in our protocol.

3. Skimming. Protein skimmers are devices that mix air and water together to create a foam. The nature of many pollutants in the marine aquarium causes them to be attracted to air bubbles, and they coat the surface of the bubbles, riding up the column of the skimmer in the foam. At the top, the foam overflows into a cup, the bubbles pop, and the pollutants accumulate as a dark gunk until you clean the cup.

4. Water Changes. Regularly removing some of the water from your aquarium and replacing it with fresh water of the proper chemistry will do more to keep your fish healthy and happy than anything else you can do. The more water you change and the more often you change it, the cleaner the water in your aquarium will be.

## Biofiltration

Biofiltration refers to filtration performed by special bacterial colonies. Before we talk more about biofiltration, let's take a quick look at the other two types of filtration. Mechanical filtration media, often polyester pads, physically trap suspended material as the water passes through them. This makes the aquarium water clearer, but since the dirt remains in the water flow, it does

## Tank Tip

It is not a good idea to rely on chemical filtration, especially when you are first starting out.

nothing to improve water quality until the filter media are cleaned. Chemical filtration media, typically activated carbon, chemically trap dissolved substances. This does temporarily improve water quality, but it is very quickly used up. The filter inserts you use may include activated carbon, which will give you a little extra margin of safety. Just don't make the mistake of thinking since you are using carbon that you don't have to worry about water quality.

Biofiltration, on the other hand, improves water quality by converting toxic substances into a much less toxic substance. The bacteria involved are cultivated by providing a vast quantity of microscopic pores over which the aquarium water is circulated. Foam sponge is a common biomedium, since it provides a lot of surface area in its pores, and water flows through it easily. Biofiltration bacteria require large amounts of oxygen as well as large surface areas. This is the reason for what is

referred to as wet-dry technology. When water drips through a porous medium, that medium stays wet, but at any given moment much of the medium is in contact with the air. These areas have only a thin film of water on them, meaning that oxygen from the air can easily dissolve into the water. This vastly increases the number of bacteria that can colonize the medium.

Ammonia is constantly produced as a waste by fish and other organisms, and it results from decomposition as well. Ammonia will quickly kill animals if it is allowed to build up in the aquarium water. One type of bacterium in a biofilter breaks down ammonia and turns it into nitrite. Nitrite is quite toxic as well, and animals cannot tolerate much of it dissolved in their water. A second type of bacterium in a biofilter break down nitrite and turn it into nitrate. Nitrate is a relatively safe substance, and animals are harmed by nitrate only with prolonged exposure or high concentrations. You should aim to keep the

*High levels of ammonia and nitrite will kill your fish.*

concentration of nitrate at a maximum of about 10 to 20 ppm.

Again we face a process which is biologically complex but very easy to understand in its aquarium application. The basics of biofiltration can be summarized as ammonia being processed into nitrite, followed by nitrite being processed into nitrate:

$$\text{Ammonia}_{\text{TOXIC}} \rightarrow \text{Nitrite}_{\text{TOXIC}} \rightarrow \text{Nitrate}_{\text{NON-TOXIC}}$$

Regular water changes will dilute nitrate, but a third type of biofiltration bacterium can reduce the concentration of nitrate as well. The process here is one of nitrate being processed into its component nitrogen and oxygen:

$$\text{Nitrate} \rightarrow \text{Nitrogen (gas)} + \text{Oxygen (gas)}$$

The bacteria break down nitrate into nitrogen and oxygen, which escape from the aquarium into the atmosphere. In contrast to the bacteria that turn ammonia and nitrite into nitrate, these bacteria live only where the oxygen levels are very low—under the sandbed or deep in the pores of live rock. In the shallower recesses, oxygen-loving bacteria thrive, so live rock and live sand provide both types of biofiltration, the one that turns ammonia into nitrate and the one that turns nitrate into nitrogen.

## Skimming

The popularity of skimming among marine aquarists of all kinds is due to its ability to remove pollutants before they break down biologically. It efficiently takes a huge assortment of noxious substances out of the aquarium water. By adjusting the flow of air and water flow through the device, you can set it to produce a thick dark foam of concentrated pollutants. When you first set up your aquarium, there will likely be very little gunk collected, but as wastes begin to build up, your skimmer will grab a lot of them before they can break down. Over time, as you improve in your husbandry techniques you will probably see a reduction in the amount of skimmate produced, giving you a visual measure of your success.

## Water Changes

Other than biofiltration and skimming, the only way you can remove accumulated pollutants, including nitrate, is by water changes. If you lived on an unpolluted tropical island, you

**SMALL FRY**

**Pain-Free Learning**
Children can learn an awful lot of science by learning to care for a marine aquarium—and it's painless!

All tanks, whether they house freshwater or saltwater fish, must have regular water changes.

What You Need to Know

could pump ocean water into your aquarium and provide an overflow to drain off the excess. You would not need any filtration, skimming, or other waste removal, as the water in your tank would constantly be renewed. In fact, some aquaculture projects do exactly this.

Unfortunately, this is rarely possible for the marine aquarist. We have to rely on filtration and water changes to keep the water in our aquariums as pristine as possible. As with freshwater aquariums, the advice about water changes in the saltwater tank is: the more, the better; the more often, the better. For most people, fresh water is either free or extremely inexpensive, but artificial salt water is a real expense. Thus you need to strike a

reasonable balance between efforts to cleanse the water in the tank (filtration, skimming, careful husbandry) and the partial replacement of the water (water changes). Sometimes in their zeal to avoid the expense of water changes aquarists wind up spending even more on complex filtration systems!

## Cycling

It would be nice to have been able to write this book without ever using the term "cycling." It is such a loaded term in aquarium circles that it is possible to discuss the concept for an entire book and not be done with it. Many new aquarists and their fish suffer unnecessarily with elaborate, almost mystical, theories and protocols for cycling an aquarium. People delve into the intricacies of a variety of biochemical processes and abstract calculations. The whole process, however, can be reduced to four important points:

1. Cycling an aquarium is another way of saying that you're letting a biofilter mature.
2. In a biofilter, bacteria convert toxic ammonia to much-less-toxic nitrate.
3. An aquarium in which a biofilter is maturing will first accumulate ammonia, then nitrite, and finally nitrate. When the biofilter is mature, only nitrate will be present.
4. When ammonia and nitrite concentrations consistently test zero, nitrate will begin to accumulate, and the aquarium is then safe for fish.

Although the filters in our protocol will provide biofiltration, when you first set up the tank they will not have any biofiltration bacteria colonizing their media. Nevertheless, you *will* be starting with a substantial biofilter—your live rock. Unfortunately, there is no way to see or to measure the extent of that biofilter. So, while your two filters mature as biofilters, you do not know how much fish waste can be processed by the live rock. This is where test kits come in.

By measuring ammonia, nitrite, and nitrate, you can gauge the maturation of your biofilter. The exact procedure for cycling your tank, or maturing your biofilter, will be covered in Chapter 4. What you need to know about cycling is that you should not pay attention to any other advice you hear about it. Do not get caught up in the mystique and confusion surrounding the very simple concept of letting your biofilter mature properly.

## Cold-Bloodedness

A very important topic to understand if you want to succeed as a marine aquarist is that of cold-bloodedness. We will discuss the implications of this

*Marine fish are ectothermic, or cold-blooded.*

further in Chapter 5, but for now we will simply define the situation. Marine fish and invertebrates are almost exclusively ectothermic, meaning that their body temperature matches that of the surrounding water very closely. This contrasts, of course, with a warm-blooded (endothermic) animal like a dog or a human, whose body temperature stays practically unchanged no matter what the temperature of the environment is.

Keeping a stable temperature has a large biological cost—warm-blooded animals expend a great deal of energy just staying warm. In fact, endotherms must consume three to ten times as much food as ectotherms of similar size and activity. The smaller the animal, the more it must eat in relative terms, since small animals lose relatively much more body heat through their skin than large animals do. Tiny mammals like shrews can starve to death if deprived of food for just a few hours. Tiny fish, on the other hand, need no food to maintain body temperature.

Likewise, the colder it gets, the more warm-blooded animals must eat to survive, since it is harder to maintain body temperature,

but as it gets colder, cold blooded animals eat less and less and finally stop eating altogether.

It is possible to underfeed a kitten, which will cause it to become frail and ill—it requires a certain amount of specific nutrients to grow properly and stay healthy. It is much harder to define underfeeding for a fish, since if it does not receive sufficient nutrients, it simply will be inactive and not grow. When it gets food, it will resume activity and growth. Prolonged starvation is of course dangerous for fish, but their natural state is to utilize food as it's available and to wait out leaner times.

## Enough is Enough

All right, enough theory. It's time to look at exactly what you'll need to set up that marine aquarium!

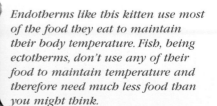

*Endotherms like this kitten use most of the food they eat to maintain their body temperature. Fish, being ectotherms, don't use any of their food to maintain temperature and therefore need much less food than you might think.*

# Chapter 3

# What You

# Need to Have

A quick trip down the aquarium aisles of your local pet or tropical fish specialty store will confirm that there are many different types of equipment sold for setting up and maintaining aquariums. The marine side of the hobby has even more types of equipment than the freshwater side. Fortunately, not all of those items are necessary for a successful first saltwater tank. For now, despite what anyone else may tell you, the equipment listed in this chapter is all you will need, and it's all you should use at first.

## The Aquarium

The single most important factor in guaranteeing success with your first marine aquarium is starting big enough. It may seem counterintuitive, but the larger your aquarium, the more likely you will be to succeed. The reason for this is simple—the number one cause of aquarist failure is dying fish; the number one cause of dying fish is poor water conditions; and the larger the volume of water you start with, the longer it takes for water conditions to deteriorate to the danger point, which gives you more time to notice the problem and fix it.

In addition, one of the most common reasons for deadly water conditions is overcrowding. It is difficult for beginning aquarists to resist all the beautiful fish in the store, so they tend to wind up buying too many. A larger tank gives you more of a buffer zone here, since the bigger the tank, the more likely it will be large enough for all the must-have specimens.

## Tank Size

Sometimes people argue in favor of a false economy, pointing out that a large tank costs many times what a smaller one does. If, however, you add up all the equipment and supplies you need, you will find that this difference diminishes rapidly. In fact, the tank itself can be one of the smaller expenses in setting up an aquarium.

So how big is big enough? The rule of thumb is that you should get the largest possible aquarium you can

*Beginners to the saltwater aquarium must show restraint when first stocking their tank. One may be inclined to purchase one colorful fish after another. Such eagerness can lead to overcrowding, which will harm all the fish in the tank.*

## Making It Work

More than half of the people who begin in the aquarium hobby abandon it within a year. In almost every case the reason is that the new aquarist is unable to keep fish alive, and after a few rounds of replacement and death, he or she gives up in frustration. Take the appropriate steps to ensure success and you will be on your way to a lifetime of enjoying this wonderful hobby.

afford and have room for, but that is nowhere near as easy to determine as it might seem. There are diehard aquarists who would think nothing of spending a month's salary on a tank that requires them to remove the sofa from the living room to make room for it. Someone else might consider a 5-gallon desktop aquarium to be an expensive intrusion. In order to put a number to our rule of thumb, we'll define the smallest tank you should consider as about 200 liters. In standard American aquarium sizes that would be either the 50-gallon or the very popular 55-gallon tank.

These might sound awfully big. They aren't really—they're comparable in size to a lot of television sets. The 50 is about 36 by 18 by 18 inches (90 by 45 by 45 cm), and the 55 is about 48 by 13 by 20 inches (140 by 35 by 50 cm). Choosing a smaller aquarium will not necessarily doom you to failure, but if you really want to succeed, try to get a tank at least this large. Despite the enormous popularity of the 55, a 50-gallon aquarium (sometimes called a 50 breeder) has a few advantages, one of which is its slightly greater surface area—of both the water at the top of the tank and the sand at the bottom of the tank. The larger bottom area gives you more room for rock and other decorations, and it gives bottom-dwelling fish more room for their territories. While your dealer will undoubtedly have 55-gallon tanks in stock, you may have to order a 50. It's worth the effort.

## 50 vs. 55

The shorter, wider configuration of a 50-gallon aquarium gives it a greater surface area than that of a 55-gallon aquarium, which is longer and narrower. The area of a 50 is 648 square inches (36 x 18) or 4.5 square feet, but a 55 has an area of 624 square inches (48 x 13) or 4.3 square feet.

## Glass or Acrylic?

Many marine hobbyists prefer acrylic tanks. They are less prone to breakage than glass tanks, and they retain heat better. They are, however, much more susceptible to scratches from routine maintenance like scraping algae off the viewing panel. Another reason marine hobbyists like acrylic is that it is simple to drill holes wherever you want them, and the elaborate plumbing designs many marine aquarists use require various points of entry into the tank. At this point you don't have to worry about that. For many people the deciding factor is that acrylic tanks cost more than glass tanks of the same size. Either type of tank will serve you very well, and you should choose whichever you prefer.

## Aquarium Stand

Salt water weighs more than 8 pounds per gallon (over a kilo per liter). When you figure in the weight of the aquarium, substrate, and rocks, you can count on a minimum of 10 to 15 pounds per gallon (1.2 to 1.8 kilos per liter) of tank capacity. That means that our recommended 50- or 55-gallon tank will tip the scales at more than a quarter of a ton (a 200-liter will weigh not 200 kilos, but a quarter to a third of a metric ton).

The only support you should consider for your aquarium is a stand or cabinet manufactured expressly to hold an aquarium of the size you will be placing on it.

*Regular furniture (tables, dressers, bookcases) are not designed to hold anything near the weight of an aquarium. Use only a stand designed specifically to hold the weight of the tank.*

This can be an utilitarian steel frame, a furniture-quality custom cabinet, or anything in between, as long as it is designed to hold the tank. Skimping in this matter is inviting tragedy.

## Aquarium Top

Like the stand, the aquarium top can be as simple as a piece of glass or plastic cut to fit or as luxurious as a furniture-quality custom canopy made to match the stand. Your aesthetic preference is the only deciding factor of importance. A top, however, is not optional. While some species of fish are notorious as jumpers, absolutely any fish can jump out to its death. The top keeps the fish in, and it keeps out things that don't belong in the tank, from dust to furry pets and little hands. It also cuts down on evaporation.

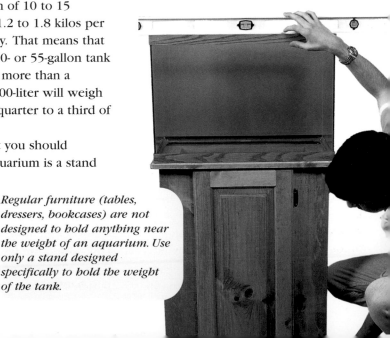

An aquarium top keeps fish from jumping out, and curious observers from getting in.

with colors so bright, so contrastive, so extensive that it is a shame to display marine tropical fish under inadequate light. You will not need the expensive, high-intensity lighting a reef aquarium with its photosynthetic invertebrates requires, but you do want to show your fish to their best advantage, and you want the coralline algae on your live rock to grow well.

The best choice is a power compact light fixture with a 96-watt bulb. A regular fluorescent double-tube strip light is an acceptable alternative, but the standard single-tube fixture will prove to be a disappointment—especially the first time you see someone else's aquarium with more intense lighting.

The simplest top is one or more pieces of glass or acrylic cut to fit the aquarium. If you choose this route, make sure that you have the edges finished. This is especially important with glass. Unless the cut edges of a piece of glass are ground down, they present a serious threat, able to cause deep lacerations with minimal contact with your skin.

## Lighting

A coral reef is a bright place. On or near the Equator it receives 12 hours of sunshine per day, sunshine that is overhead all year long. The animals on the reef have evolved to take full advantage of all that insolation. Although scientists are not sure why coral reef fish are so vibrantly colorful, the fact remains that the reef teems

## Air Pump

This is an exception, since the protocol includes a piece of equipment that you will not be using on a regular basis. Many non-aquarists relate an air pump to an aquarium and find it difficult to believe it is not a necessary item. There's nothing wrong with air pumps; they simply do not figure in the aquarium setup outlined in this simple protocol for success. You will need a small air pump only for your quarantine tank (discussed later in this chapter).

## Filtration

All aquariums need filtration, but they don't all need filters. Live rock and live sand perform significant filtration, and protein skimmers eliminate the need for some filtration. When used together without any other filter, they constitute what is often called the modified Berlin system for marine setups. For a variety of reasons, our protocol here calls for filters as well: two hang-on power filters.

The brand and the exact design of the filters you choose are not important, but they should have a wet-dry biofiltration capability. We will explain what that means later on in this chapter. For now we'll simply point out that a hang-on filter normally has compartments that hold various filter media. The water from the tank flows through these compartments and then back into the aquarium. A filter with wet-dry biofiltration will have a non-submerged medium as the last step in the water's return. The two most common designs are a rotating biowheel, which stays wet via a spraybar while slowly turning in the air, and a suspended sponge compartment just above the tank's water line, through which the water drips before returning to the aquarium. Any design that includes a porous medium exposed to the air through which the water passes will perform the appropriate wet-dry biofiltration.

The water pump integral to the filters should be rated to move water at six tank volumes per hour. For our 50/55-gallon, that means about 300 gallons per hour (for 200 liters, 1,200 liters per hour). You will be running two of these filters on your aquarium.

## Protein Skimmer

You need a protein skimmer that uses a water pump, not one that is air driven. The skimmer mixes air and water to create bubbles. The bubbles rise through a cylinder through which the aquarium water is pumped. The bubbles make use of a process known as foam fractionation

## A Peek Behind the Curtain

We said we weren't going to explain all of our choices, but you may be wondering why the protocol calls for two filters. Some of the reasons include providing sufficient water flow, preventing excessive bacterial loss during cleaning, avoiding the need for powerheads, and maximizing gas exchange. It's okay if you don't know what all that means. That's why this book makes it so easy to succeed with a marine aquarium—we've taken care of the details behind the scenes.

A protein skimmer is just one tool needed to create a clean, healthy tank for your fish.

(don't need to know) to remove many contaminants before they have a chance to break down and pollute your aquarium water (do need to know). These contaminants stick chemically to the bubbles, rising up the column and frothing over into a doughnut-shaped collection cup that sits at the top of the cylinder; the cleansed water returns to the tank. When the air and water flow are adjusted properly, the foam will cause a dark brown gunk to accumulate. When the cup is mostly full, you'll need to dump it down a drain, clean the cup, and replace it.

Again specific brand or design is not important. Get a skimmer rated for a tank at least as large as yours; larger is fine. Your dealer can go over the various features with you to help you make your choice. Since our protocol does not call for a sump or for a wet-dry filter (not the same thing as a power filter with a wet-dry component), you will need a skimmer that hangs on the tank and draws water directly from the aquarium. Make sure you ask for this type.

## Heater

The temperature on a coral reef does not vary very much. Day in and day out, throughout the year, the water is always about 78° to 80°F (26° to 27°C). A reliable heater is needed to maintain the proper temperature in your aquarium. Depending on how cool the room in which the aquarium will be located gets, you will need a heater of 150 to 200 watts. If you elect to set up a larger aquarium than the minimum suggested (great!), figure about 3 watts per gallon (about 1.5 watts for every 2 liters).

Allowing the water temperature to get too high can be as dangerous to your fish as chilling. If you live in a particularly hot climate and do not have air conditioning to keep the room within a few degrees of 80°F (27°C), you will have to make provisions to cool the aquarium. One way of doing this is to position a fan to blow across the surface of the water. (You will therefore have to replace the usual cover with a plastic grid or mesh.) This increases evaporation, which cools the water. If that is insufficient, you will need to either invest in a chiller for the aquarium or buy an air conditioner for the room—in which case you and your family can also benefit!

## Measuring Devices

There are four types of measurements that you will have to make to monitor the condition of your aquarium on a regular basis, so you will need to purchase the tools required to make these measurements.

### Temperature

To monitor your aquarium's temperature, you will need a thermometer. Although there are such high-tech devices as electronic

thermometers and wireless infra-red meters that you simply point at your aquarium to read the water temperature, an inexpensive liquid crystal thermometer that sticks on the outside of the glass is perfectly adequate.

### Salinity

Another measurement you will need to make is that of salinity, of how much salt is dissolved in the water. There are a variety of devices to measure this, but an inexpensive swing-arm plastic hydrometer is adequate. For an extra expense, you can get a refractometer, which offers far greater precision and reliability.

### pH Test Kit

We've already discussed how a drop in pH indicates a problem in a marine aquarium. A simple pH test kit enables you to monitor pH. The easiest to use

*pH test kits are available and will allow you to monitor your tank's levels.*

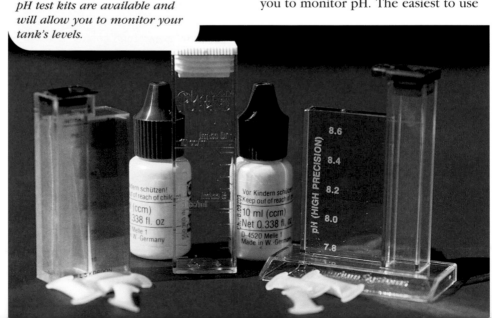

## Hands Off!

Since the equipment for your marine aquarium is literally life-support equipment, it is vital that you teach your children from the start that they cannot touch any of it. This will protect your child as well as your aquarium.

is a test strip, which you dip into a sample of the water. You then compare the color on the strip to the chart provided to determine the pH. A test kit designed for marine aquarium use will be able to read the high (as compared to freshwater aquariums) pH values needed.

### Nitrogen Test Kits

Depending on the available products, you may need one, two, or three kits to test for the important components of the nitrogen cycle in your aquarium: ammonia, nitrite, and nitrate. You will need these tests while your aquarium is cycling, when you first set it up. After that, you may need to use them from time to time to pinpoint a problem, but their principal use will be in the beginning.

## Water

You might think it strange that I list water in a discussion of things you need to procure. Most serious marine aquarists do not use their tap water for their tanks. They usually use purified water, often produced by a reverse osmosis device intended for home use. The idea behind this is that a marine aquarist goes to considerable effort and expense to get the chemistry of the water just right. In light of this, why start with water that already has a complex chemistry? By using pure water, the desired goal is achieved.

Our protocol here, however, calls for using tap water to mix up artificial sea water if possible. This is in keeping with our minimalist approach to aquarium water chemistry. At the level of precision we are seeking, the use of tap water will suffice in almost all cases. If you are aware of gross abnormalities in your water supply—such as its being unsuitable for drinking—you will want to find an alternative source for any aquarium you might set up, marine or not.

Using your test kits, check your tap water. If it contains ammonia or nitrite, you should not use it for your aquarium (and probably not for yourself, either!). High nitrates are a problem in well water in some agricultural areas. If your water has measurable nitrates, you should not use it for your aquarium. Some tap water has measurable phosphates. If yours does, you may find that no matter what you do your tank is shrouded in algae. In any of these cases, buying reverse-osmosis water or purchasing a reverse-osmosis unit and producing your own are your only viable options. Do not be intimidated by all this. The vast majority of tap waters should prove acceptable.

*Be sure to treat your tap water to remove sanitizers like chlorine and chloramine.*

### Dechloraminator

Unless your tap provides untreated well water, your water has a sanitizer added, typically chlorine, chloramine, or a mixture of the two. These chemicals are dangerous to marine life and need to be neutralized. Simple aging or brisk agitation will drive chlorine out of the water, but chloramine is much more persistent (the major reason it is used). Plain chlorine neutralizers will remove the chlorine from chloramine, but this leaves ammonia, which is of course also toxic. To further complicate matters, many municipal water supplies alternate between the two sanitizers, so an aquarist has no way of knowing what is in his or her water. The only safe approach is to treat your water with a chlorine and chloramine neutralizer, usually referred to as a dechloraminator. This neutralizes both the chlorine and the ammonia.

### Mixing Tub

You need some way of mixing up and storing salt water. Large plastic buckets or small garbage cans are the typical choices, but plastic stock tanks and even spare aquariums are fine. Only containers made of glass or food-grade plastic are acceptable; metal cannot be used. You should also get a submersible heater rated for the number of gallons and a powerhead. A powerhead is a small submersible water pump that is often attached to various types of filters. In this case just drop it into the tub to provide circulation and mixing.

## Water Softeners

If your water supply goes through a household water softener, it is preferable to bypass the softener to obtain water for your aquarium, but if this is not possible, do not worry.

## Buckets

You will need at least one 5-gallon (19-liter) plastic bucket. This may come in handy for many things, but it will be vital for acclimation and water changes. You should buy a new bucket to make sure it has never been used with any chemicals or detergents. Mark the bucket prominently so that no one else uses it for anything other than aquarium purposes.

## Salt Mix

You need a high-quality salt mix. It is vital that you understand that this means a mix of many different salts. It is certainly possible to mix up a solution of table salt (sodium chloride) with a specific gravity of 1.025. Marine fish placed into this solution would not die immediately, but they would be under extreme stress, and they would not survive long. Marine invertebrates would die even more quickly. The difference between that "salt water"

### Need to Know?

You need to know what you don't need to know. Huh?

Here's what you don't need to know: a salt is *a compound in which some or all of the hydrogen ions in an acid are replaced with metal ions or with electropositive radicals*. Here's what you need to know: the "salt" in "salt water" is not table salt.

and seawater is like the difference between a bowl of flour and a cake. Table salt is a major component of seawater, but it requires many other components to produce a solution in which marine organisms can thrive.

If you understand this, you will understand that it is possible for various salt mixes to differ in composition, to differ in how closely they mimic natural sea water. Because of the complexities of the chemistry of salts it is even possible for two salt mixes with the same ingredient lists to differ in the quality of the sea water they produce. You should follow the advice of your local retailer in choosing a brand of salt mix.

*Plastic buckets can serve a variety of uses.*

## Keep It Dry!

Salt mix will absorb water out of the air, which can cause it to harden into lumps. This not only makes it harder to dissolve the mix but also changes its chemical nature, and water formulated with hardened salt mix will not have the proper chemical makeup. Keep the mix in an airtight container and make sure to close it up immediately after using it.

## Acclimation Kit

You will use your acclimation kit only when you get a new fish and bring it home. Fortunately, an acclimation kit is very simple and inexpensive. All you need is a length of airline tubing, about 8 feet (2.5 m), a plastic air valve, and a couple of clothespins. We will discuss how to assemble the kit in Chapter 7.

## Live Rock

Live rock is a critical component of a successful marine aquarium. No, not every aquarium has to have live rock, but it makes it a lot easier to succeed, and it also makes the aquarium look natural and beautiful. In addition, it provides a natural environment for fish, many of which live in the spaces between the rocks and graze on organisms that grow on and among the rock. Our protocol calls for its use. In fact, live rock provides major filtration for the setup. But what is live rock? The nearly oxymoronic phrase "live rock" refers to coralline rock that is full of living organisms. These porous skeletons of hard corals were once thriving coral colonies, but after the corals died the rock became encrusted with various algae, and its pores

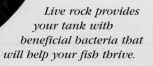

*Live rock provides your tank with beneficial bacteria that will help your fish thrive.*

*Because of all the organisms living on, in, and among the pieces of live rock and in live sand, it has to be treated like a living thing, especially for shipping. There will be some die-off during shipping, so when live rock first arrives, it has to be cured or cycled. That is a procedure not to be undertaken by a beginning aquarist, so you should buy live rock fully cured from your local retailer.*

were colonized by bacteria. The deeper into the rock a pore goes, the less oxygen there will be; near the surface are oxygen-loving bacteria, further in there are bacteria that do well in low-oxygen environments, and deep within the rock are bacteria that live without oxygen. Live rock is almost always harvested from the ocean. It may be naturally occurring pieces that break off in storms and collect in rubble zones, or it may be aquacultured live rock, which is coral limestone rock that is barged out to sea and dumped. After several years it is covered with life and ready to be used.

## Life on Live Rock

The bacteria and encrusting algae on live rock are extremely important, but not all the life on live rock is microscopic. Macroalgae and sessile invertebrates like corals and sponges are sometimes found on the rock, and even more often they appear on the rock some time after it is placed into an aquarium. Tiny crustaceans called amphipods and copepods usually show up in piles of live rock, and even larger invertebrates like worms, shrimp, and crabs often come out of crevices in the rock.

## How Much Live Rock Do I Need?

In part how much rock you need depends on the density of the rock. Lighter rock requires fewer pounds per gallon than heavier rock does. The usual recommendation for a reef tank is about two pounds per gallon capacity of the aquarium. You can certainly get about 100 pounds (45 kg) of live rock, but our protocol calls for only 40 to 50 pounds (20 kg). This amount will provide good biofiltration and a nice aquascaping. You will not be able to build as large a "reef" of rock as you would with twice the amount of rock, but as cured live rock is quite expensive, buying fewer pounds of it will save you a considerable amount of money.

## Live Sand

Like live rock, live sand houses a variety of organisms: bacteria and tiny worms, crustaceans, starfish, and mollusks. Sources for quality live sand are harder to find than those for live rock, but it is fairly easy to make your own live sand. Aragonite sand and/or crushed coral is the best substrate for your aquarium. You want a 1- to 3-inch (2- to 7-cm) bed of sand on the bottom of your tank. You can then add a few handfuls of sand from an established marine tank—a friend's, or your local dealer's. This will introduce live sand organisms, including bacteria, that will soon reproduce and populate the entire sandbed. If you find a source for live sand, you can certainly use that for part or all of your sandbed, in which case you won't have to wait for the sand to be fully populated.

## Quarantine Tank

You will need a quarantine tank. It does not need to be very big—10 or 20 gallons (50 to 75 liters) will be fine. You'll need a 100-watt heater, a well-fitting top (which can be just a piece of acrylic or glass cut to fit), a small sponge filter, and a small air pump to run the filter. You do not need a light. The tank should be bare bottomed, with no substrate. You will use this tank primarily when you purchase a new fish. We will discuss its proper use in Chapter 7.

## Water-Change Equipment

Water changes can be performed with the time-honored bucket and siphon hose. The bucket used must be plastic, and it cannot be used for anything other than the aquarium, as traces of detergents or cleaners will kill your livestock. The minimum length for the hose or tubing is long enough to reach from the bottom of the aquarium to within the bucket on the floor, but it will save you a lot of effort if you purchase tubing long enough to reach a convenient drain. This can be a floor drain or a sink or toilet; it must, of course, be lower than the level of the aquarium.

While it is possible to refill your aquarium by taking bucketfuls of water from your mixing tub to the tank, this chore can be avoided through use of a fitting that attaches your tubing to the powerhead in the tub. When you are ready to refill the tank, just hook the siphon hose to the powerhead, and it becomes a refill hose!

## Miscellaneous Equipment

Net—You will need at least one fish net for occasions on which you must move a fish.

Algae scraper—This will enable you to clean algae off the front pane of the aquarium. A metal blade can be used on glass, but an acrylic tank requires the use of a special plastic blade.

## Things You Need to Have

- 50- or 55-gallon aquarium
- aquarium stand
- aquarium top
- double-bulb fluorescent or power compact light fixture
- two 300-gph hang-on filters with wet-dry components
- hang-on protein skimmer
- 150- to 200-watt submersible heater
- thermometer
- hydrometer or refractometer
- test kits for pH, ammonia, nitrite, and nitrate
- water (only if your tap water is unacceptable)
- dechloraminator
- mixing tub, including powerhead and submersible heater
- at least one plastic bucket
- salt mix
- acclimation kit, including one plastic air valve and a length of airline tubing
- 40 to 50 pounds fully cured live rock
- substrate—crushed coral or aragonite sand
- quarantine tank, including sponge filter, air pump, and 100-watt heater
- water-change (siphoning) equipment
- net
- algae scraper

# Chapter 4

# What You

# Need
# to Do

Okay, now you know what you need to know and what you need to have. In this chapter we'll spell out what you need to do to set up your aquarium and maintain it.

## Mixing Up Salt Water

What can be so hard about mixing up salt water that our protocol needs instructions for it? Well, it isn't hard, but it should be done correctly. You should never mix the water in the aquarium itself, and you should never use water immediately after you mix it up. This is because even if it appears that all of the salt mix has dissolved, the process continues at the microscopic level. You need to wait at least a few hours to be sure that the water composition is correct.

Begin by filling the mixing tub with water; it is important to keep track of how much water you put in. Turn on the powerhead to get the water circulating. Then add the amount of salt mix indicated by the manufacturer (usually 1/2 cup for each gallon). This will give you water with approximately the correct salinity. You must wait for the salt to completely dissolve, and for the water to come up to temperature, before testing the specific gravity with your hydrometer. So, plug in the heater and let everything swirl for a few hours. Then check the salinity; you may well find it is between 1.024 and 1.026, which means it is ready to use.

If you find the specific gravity low, you should add a little salt mix, then check it again. Although it is best to wait a couple of hours, the amount of salt added is quite small, and just waiting until the salt is visibly gone is adequate. If the specific gravity is high,

## Tank Tips

- Never mix the salt water in the aquarium. Never use water immediately after mixing it up. Wait a few hours to make sure the water composition is correct.
- You should not add water to salt mix in the bucket. The initial high concentrations can cause chemicals in the mix to react in adverse ways, making the final solution different from the way it should be. By adding the salt mix to a bucket of water, you prevent this from happening.
- It is a good idea to always have the mixing tub full for emergency water changes.

add a small amount of water, then check again. Repeat the process until you get a reading of about 1.025. The water is now ready for use.

## Building the Reef

The first step in setting up a marine aquarium is to fill it between 50 and 75 percent with properly mixed artificial sea water at the proper temperature of between 78° and 80°F (26° to 27°C) so the live rock will not dry out. Plug in the heater to maintain the temperature. You should have the rest of the water you will need ready in your mixing tub.

You are then ready to add the rock. The reason you start with the rock and later add the sand is that it is vital to build a secure structure that cannot be undermined by fish digging in the sand. When the large base rocks rest firmly right on the bottom glass, no amount of excavation can topple them. As you build up the "reef" of rocks, leave plenty of open spaces, caves, and holes. Aside from providing animals with places to hide, this ensures good water circulation, which is vital to the biofiltration capabilities of the rock. Make sure that each level is completely stable before building upwards.

The exact configuration of the rocks will depend on their particular shapes and your sense of aesthetics. You may want to consider some of the most popular configuration plans in deciding how you want your tank to look. Some of these might require more rock than you have, so you can modify them to fit your circumstances.

## Back Wall

The entire back wall of the aquarium is piled with rocks, getting narrower as it goes up. This leaves the entire front of the tank unobstructed, and the fish can swim from one side to the other along the front glass and pop into and out of holes in the rock wall the whole way.

## Flanking Columns

The rocks are piled high at both ends of the tank, with the space in between open. You'll wind up with fish taking up residence in holes in both rockpiles and swimming freely between them.

## U-Shape

In this configuration the space between the two columns is filled with rock, but not piled very high. Fish can also set up home in crevices in the rocks on the bottom in the middle, but most of the center space is still open for swimming.

## Full Tank

This is like the back wall setup, only the first layer stretches from the front glass to the back.

*The setup you choose has to appeal to your aesthetics, but remember, your fish have to live it in. Make sure you leave enough room for them to move around.*

What You Need to Do

## Why Only Partially Filled?

The reason to start with the aquarium only half to three-quarters full is that as you add the rock and sand, the water level will rise. If you fill the tank first, it will overflow as you stack the live rock.

The entire pile narrows to the back as it rises, leaving some open space and stabilizing the rockpile. This approach is often favored by reef aquarists, since it maximizes the ability to place invertebrates at different levels.

### Center Island

The image evoked here is of a pyramidal mount rising from the seafloor—a pile of live rock in the center of the aquarium, with sand all around.

### Sandbed

Once the rock formation suits you, you can add the sand. It will have particles of all sizes, down to mere dust. This

*Notice that the rock is not piled very high, leaving plenty of room in the tank for fish to move about.*

An example of the full tank layout.

can cause the tank to become quite cloudy. Normally the particles will settle quickly, but if there seems to be excessive dust in the sand, you can rinse it first.

People use various methods to minimize cloudiness and keep the sand off the live rock. A piece of plastic pipe fitted with a funnel can be used to precisely direct the sand. Another method is to put the sand in a bowl or pitcher, gently lower it into the water, and then pour the sand out just above the bottom.

Once the rocks and the substrate are in place, you can fill the aquarium with mixed water and start the filters.

Before you can add any fish, the tank must be cycled. Remember the four points of cycling from Chapter 2:

1. Cycling an aquarium is another way of saying letting a biofilter mature.
2. In a biofilter, bacteria convert toxic ammonia to much-less-toxic nitrate.
3. An aquarium in which a biofilter is maturing will first accumulate ammonia, then nitrite, and finally nitrate. When it is mature, only nitrate will be present.
4. When ammonia and nitrite concentrations consistently test zero, nitrate will begin to accumulate, and the aquarium is then safe for fish.

Our protocol calls for what is known as cycling with live rock. This is actually better described as installing a biofilter in the form of cured live rock. If you have gotten fully cured rock, you should have an instant biofilter in your tank. You must rely on your dealer, since you cannot tell how well cured the rock is just by looking at it. Make sure that you specify that you need live rock that will not need further curing.

Test the water in the aquarium a few hours after you add the rock.

## Territoriality

The importance of territoriality must be kept in mind as you build up rock. When it comes to fish territories, very often out of sight does indeed mean out of mind. Creating visual barriers so that a fish staking out a territory in the rockpile cannot see the other end of the tank helps keep the peace.

It should register zero for ammonia, nitrite, and nitrate. Test again the next day. If you again get three zeroes, you should be able to start stocking the tank.

You want to stock gradually, to make sure the biofilter expands to keep up with the increased waste production. Ideally, therefore, you add a few fish, check for ammonia and nitrite for a couple days, and if there are no spikes of either, then you can add a few more fish, and so on. There is a problem, however…

## Quarantine Compromise

Here you face a dilemma. All fish should be quarantined before being placed into your tank. You might argue that since there aren't any fish in the main tank the fish added can't make any other fish sick. The problem with that line of thinking is that the fish may be about to come down with an illness. If this happens, the aquarium becomes infected. You can't treat the fish in there without damaging live rock organisms, and you would have to run the tank for half a year without any fish to make sure that you have eradicated all pathogens! On the other hand, the little sponge filter in your quarantine tank has no biofilter in it, while your main tank has a mature biofilter in the live rock. This means that fish in your quarantine tank could die of ammonia

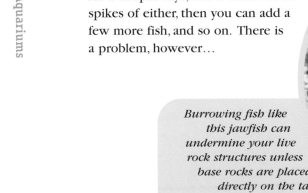

*Burrowing fish like this jawfish can undermine your live rock structures unless base rocks are placed directly on the tank bottom glass.*

SMALL FRY

## Good Job!

Involving your kids in the setup of your marine aquarium will give them a sense of accomplishment once they see the fish thriving in the tank.

poisoning but wouldn't in the main aquarium. For a full discussion on quarantine, see Chapter 7.

Our protocol calls for the following compromises for the initial stocking of the aquarium:

If possible, select your fish and ask your retailer to keep them for a couple of weeks. If you have bought all of your equipment and live rock from them, they should be agreeable to this. In fact, you can select your fish when you buy your aquarium and let this "store quarantine" period start while you are setting everything up. While this time interval is not the full life-cycle period for all pathogens, most diseases will show up in two or three weeks.

Whether you are able to do this or not, bring your fish home a few at a time, and give the fish a freshwater dip when you get them home (see Chapter 7). This simple action can prevent disasters, as it can cause any parasites to release their hold and drop off the fish.

Include a few cleaners (see Chapter 6) in your initial stocking—peppermint shrimp, neon gobies, etc. If any parasites slip through, these animals should literally nip them in the bud.

Make sure that you check ammonia and nitrite daily after adding any fish, and wait several days at the minimum before adding any more. If you get a spike of either, keep an eye on the levels, and if they go into the danger zone, do a partial water change to

*Treating sick fish in your main tank may compromise the healthy bacteria in your live rock, hence the need for a quarantine tank.*

What You Need to Do

Lysmata amboinensis, *a cleaner shrimp.*

dilute them to safe levels. With cycled live rock, if you only add only a couple of fish at a time, you should be fine.

## Regular Maintenance

Once your tank is up and running, you will need to begin regular maintenance. It is especially important to check on your setup daily. Many tragic problems begin slowly and can be averted if caught early. The time schedules that follow are suggestions. Circumstance may dictate performing certain maintenance procedures more or less frequently than indicated here.

## Daily Maintenance

You will be feeding your fish at least once a day. Whenever you go to your aquarium, you should check it quickly. Is the temperature correct? A slight rise or drop in temperature won't harm your fish, but it could alert you to failure of the heater or to some other problem. You can then remedy the problem before a large rise or drop kills your fish. Are the filters operating properly? A filter that has lost its prime and is running dry will quickly burn out. Impeded return flow indicates dirty medium or some other obstruction. Also check the skimmer to see whether it needs adjustment or emptying.

## Weekly/Biweekly Maintenance

### Water

Weekly water changes are a good idea. Even more frequent changes are great, and less frequent changes are better than none. Weekly salinity and pH checks are also in order. If the water level drops from evaporation, you should add replacement (in this case fresh) water.

## Skimmer

The skimmer will probably need cleaning every one or two weeks. This is in addition to emptying the collection cup. When slime builds up on the inner parts, skimming efficiency drops. A soft cloth or paper towel should easily shine them up, and you can rinse them in fresh water. Make certain you never use any soaps or cleansers on any aquarium equipment.

## Filters

Chances are that your power filters will have at least two compartments for media. With two filters, that means at least four separate compartments. If you clean or replace one per week, then in a month or so you will have completely cleaned the filters. It is important to change filter media

*Overfeeding, as in humans, causes health problems in fish. Not only that, but any uneaten food will decompose and foul the tank's water.*

## Watch Your Fish

The most enjoyable part of aquarium keeping is getting to know your fish. Take the time to simply watch them. Not only will you appreciate them more, you will be learning what their normal appearance and behavior is. This makes it easier to detect when something is wrong.

gradually, since even though they are not part of the wet-dry biofilter, regular filter media provide a lot of biofiltration. By cleaning or replacing only one set at a time, you avoid a sudden loss of biofiltration capacity.

## Clean the Glass

If you can't see your fish easily, you cannot enjoy them. Weekly cleaning of the glass may be necessary to keep your view unobstructed. When you first set up the tank, a brown film may form on the glass. This is caused by a bloom of algae. It generally diminishes quickly and disappears, but it can be annoying at first. An algae scraper should make quick work of any growth, which depending on the conditions in the tank can be brown, red, green, or another in color.

I encourage you to allow algae to grow on all panes that are not used for viewing. In most setups this includes the back and both ends. Algae growing on the glass are

What You Need to Do

using up nutrients that otherwise could fuel growth on your live rock. If they are permitted to grow on the glass, they will be less likely to colonize the rock. Many fish and invertebrates like to eat algae and other organisms that grow with algae. By permitting growth where it is not in the way, you provide a salad bar at which your livestock can always snack.

At first you may object to the various films and slimes that coat the inside surfaces of your aquarium, and they admittedly are not always the nicest things to look at. Over time, however, if you do not scrape the glass

## Know Your Algae

While coralline algae is desirable on the rock, green algae and the brown or red types caused by diatoms, dinoflagellates, and cyanobacteria are not.

clean, the red or purple coralline algae that give live rock its color will spread onto all surfaces, including the tank panes. Most aquarists find it aesthetically pleasing to have this bright growth, which usually keeps other algae from taking hold. Thus, by cleaning only the viewing pane(s), you will ultimately have a nicer-looking tank.

## Monthly Maintenance

Once a month you should check all the uninteresting parts of your setup. Inspect all the equipment, make certain all electrical plugs are fully inserted, be sure there are no leaks. If you haven't already done it this month, take the top off the aquarium and clean it of streaks or salt creep.

## Evaporation and Salt Creep

The salinity in your aquarium will not remain steady. Water is lost through evaporation, increasing the salinity, since the salts remain behind as the

*Lightbulbs will need to be changed, but not nearly as frequently as the tank's water.*

## Just Water

Only water evaporates from your aquarium. All the salts remain behind. This means that the salinity in the tank increases as water is lost. Therefore you should refill the tank with fresh water, not mixed salt water.

water goes off as vapor. Salts are lost through a process known as salt creep. This refers to the gradual depositing of a crust of salt on surfaces outside the aquarium. The water that sprays or splashes onto the tank rim or cover is salt water, so as the drops dry, the water evaporates and the salts are left as a thin crust.

Both these processes are gradual, and the salinity may not change appreciably between water changes. You should check the salinity at least once a week to keep tabs on it. If it increases, top off the tank with fresh water, not mixed salt water. It is uncommon for there to be enough salt creep to decrease the salinity significantly, as water is also lost, especially since regular evaporation is also constantly offsetting it. Salt creep tends to minimize the increase in salinity from evaporation. If the dry salt falls back into the tank, however, it can add to a salinity increase.

### As-Needed Maintenance

The only other common maintenance chores are very infrequent—replacing light bulbs and repairing or replacing equipment as needed. An aquarium can run for years, even decades, with minimal fuss. Just keep up with water changes, proper filtration, and good husbandry, and you will enjoy your marine fish tank for a long time.

# Chapter 5

# Eating Well

Different coral reef species make use of a vast variety of foods, from detritus to algae, coral polyps to plankton, tiny invertebrates to other fish. Quite a few serve as cleaners. These small fish set up stations to which large fish will come for a cleaning—the little fish zip all over their clients, picking up dead skin, parasites, even bits of food trapped in their teeth! They are normally safe from predation, and they even enter the gills and mouths of fish large enough to swallow them whole.

**B**ut what about in your aquarium? Can you supply the range of nutrition that the natural reef provides? Yes, as long as you can get your fish to eat the foods available. This is largely guaranteed if you purchase tank-raised specimens. With wild-caught fishes, it is much more likely if you stick to the fish we recommend. There are many beautiful fishes that are unfortunately readily available in the trade despite the fact that they almost never adapt to aquarium foods. One of the criteria used in selecting our protocol's recommended fishes is their adaptability to captive diets.

## Commercial Foods

There is an enormous variety of commercially prepared foods for fish, many specifically formulated for marine species. This is important because the nutritional needs of saltwater species are different from those of freshwater species. While dry foods are popular and easy to use, many wild-caught marines need to be trained to eat them, and some never will accept them. Frozen and freeze-dried foods are more readily accepted, and most marines can be weaned onto them. Difficult specimens may need to be fed live foods, weaned onto frozen, then further weaned onto dry.

## Dry

Dry foods are available in flakes and in several extruded forms: pellets, sticks, and wafers. The pellets come in a range of sizes from mini to jumbo, suitable for just about any fish. Sticks are popular for feeding large predators like lionfish and groupers, but our protocol doesn't allow such huge specimens. Wafers are designed for bottom feeders, but freshwater bottom feeders are more likely than marines to accept them. Many marine aquarists favor them for feeding invertebrates like shrimp.

If you can get your fish to eat dry foods, that is great, as they provide a wide array of nutrients. With so many kinds, you can vary what you feed,

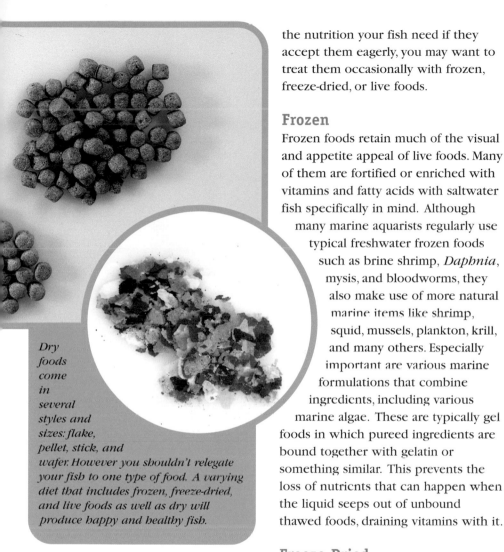

the nutrition your fish need if they accept them eagerly, you may want to treat them occasionally with frozen, freeze-dried, or live foods.

## Frozen

Frozen foods retain much of the visual and appetite appeal of live foods. Many of them are fortified or enriched with vitamins and fatty acids with saltwater fish specifically in mind. Although many marine aquarists regularly use typical freshwater frozen foods such as brine shrimp, *Daphnia*, mysis, and bloodworms, they also make use of more natural marine items like shrimp, squid, mussels, plankton, krill, and many others. Especially important are various marine formulations that combine ingredients, including various marine algae. These are typically gel foods in which pureed ingredients are bound together with gelatin or something similar. This prevents the loss of nutrients that can happen when the liquid seeps out of unbound thawed foods, draining vitamins with it.

## Freeze-Dried

From fishes' reaction to them, freeze-dried foods retain quite a bit of the appeal of frozen or live foods. At the same time, they are much more convenient to store and use. The freeze drying process also preserves most of the nutrition. Most freeze-dried

*Dry foods come in several styles and sizes: flake, pellet, stick, and wafer. However you shouldn't relegate your fish to one type of food. A varying diet that includes frozen, freeze-dried, and live foods as well as dry will produce happy and healthy fish.*

which both ensures proper nutrition and prevents your fish from being habituated to only one favorite food. If your fish ignore or pay little attention to dry foods, you will need to try frozen and freeze-dried products, and even though dry foods can provide all

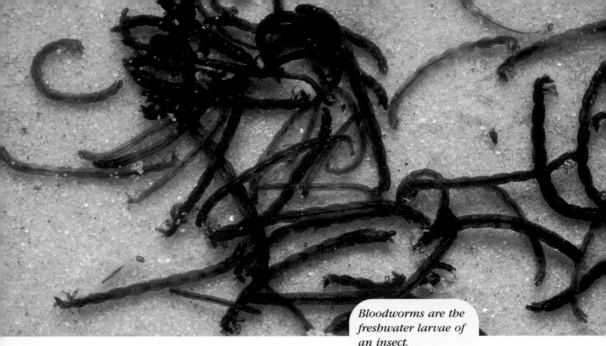

Bloodworms are the freshwater larvae of an insect.

foods are single food organisms—bloodworms, brine shrimp, krill, etc.

## Live Foods

Most marine fish will appreciate chasing down live adult brine shrimp, and newly hatched brine shrimp are often fed to invertebrates and small fishes. A more significant source of live foods in the marine aquarium, however, is the food items associated with live rock and live sand.

In the absence of severe predation, invertebrates will colonize live rock and live sand. From just small to microscopic, these worms, crustaceans, and other animals scavenge detritus (fish waste and other debris) and nibble on algae, cleaning the tank and keeping the sand stirred. They also provide meals for fish that are micropredators who pick the creatures off the rock and out of the sand. These tiny animals also may spawn in the aquarium, producing large quantities of microscopic, planktonic larvae. Most cannot be raised to maturity in the aquarium, but these larvae are greedily eaten by small fish. In a mature tank with plenty of live rock, these live foods can be a significant contribution to your fish's diet, but unfortunately, on the other hand, a few intensely predatory fish can wipe out these animals.

## Feeding Problems

There are three common problems when it comes to feeding marine fish in captivity. The first two are caused by the aquarist and are therefore easily avoidable. The last one is the fish's fault, and it may or may not be solvable.

## Overfeeding

More beginning aquarists fail because of overfeeding than for any other reason. It is bad when fish overeat, but the greater problem comes from overfeeding the aquarium. Uneaten food settles into the rocks and substrate, where it rots. In a marine aquarium this can quickly cause a total crash, as the alkalinity is used up, the pH plummets, and toxic ammonia builds up.

Even if you do not feed your fish more than they can consume, providing too much food is still a problem. First, overfed fish, like overfed people, can develop health problems associated with obesity. More immediately, overfed fish produce an excess of wastes, and the wastes can overwhelm your tank and your filtration.

Sometimes there is little you can do. Large predators are often given infrequent, but large meals, which leads to intermittent production of a lot of waste. In this case, the aquarist makes a water change a day or two after the big meal to counteract the increased waste output. Our protocol, however, does not call for any large predators, so you only have to concern yourself with less extreme cases.

The frustrating thing about this is that it is extremely difficult to explain to someone how much food should be fed. You may come across various rules of thumb, but they are woefully imprecise and misleading. The problem is made even worse by the fish themselves. Fish in the wild rarely if ever find themselves in a situation in which they can eat all they want. Instead, they are always watchful for the next feeding opportunity and how to exploit it before another fish does. This means that fish do not have elaborate natural mechanisms to stop feeding. In an aquarium they will learn to beg at the glass for food, and they will continue to beg and to feed long after they have eaten sufficiently.

*Brine shrimp will be eagerly devoured by most fish.*

# How to Feed a Finicky Feeder

Very often a fish on the reef has an extremely specific diet—say, live sponges or coral polyps—that cannot be provided in captivity. If you are unable to coax the fish into trying other food items, it will starve to death. The problem here is largely one of perception; the fish simply doesn't recognize the strange objects as food. Once that hurdle is passed, the fish comes to associate the keeper with the arrival of food; at that point the fish has adjusted to captivity and will probably continue to be an eager feeder. There are three major perceptions that entice a fish to get over the hurdle and eat something: movement, flavor/odor, and seeing other fish eat it. You can manipulate all of these to tempt a finicky feeder.

For fish that do not see immobile things as food, you can impale a strip of fish meat onto a long skewer or tie it loosely to a string and dangle the food in front of the fish to tempt the animal to strike. This often works with predatory fish that tend to hunt by sight. Soon they will be eager to grab anything you drop into the tank.

Certain foods seem to draw fish in with their odor or taste. One that often overcomes a wild-caught fish's reluctance to eat aquarium foods is a well-rinsed raw clam on the half shell. Getting a fish to take that first bite is the hardest part, and a clam often does the trick. Another food with powerful chemical attractants is krill. These marine crustaceans are real fish candy.

Fish are always interested when they see other fish feeding. If you have a specimen in a quarantine tank and it refuses all foods, you might want to place another fish in with it. Seeing its tankmate getting all the food might be all it takes to jumpstart the fish to feed.

In extreme cases aquarists have sometimes been successful using traditional freshwater live foods to tempt marine specimens—blackworms, earthworms, mosquito larvae, etc. These foods are inappropriate as a permanent diet, but they sometimes get a reluctant feeder started.

When all of this fails, there is little hope. Public aquaria with veterinarians on staff sometimes force-feed hopeless cases with a stomach tube, but even with such extreme measures the fish often fail to begin feeding. This is why our protocol stresses seeing the fish eat before purchasing it.

So how much do you feed? The only certain answer is: a lot less than you think. Take a look at your fish's eyes. Their stomachs are about the size of their eyes—or smaller. Take a look at your pellets or flakes or freeze-dried plankton. How much would it take to fill one stomach? All the stomachs? Now take whatever that much is and halve it. That isn't much food, but it's probably more than you should feed.

In fact, start by taking half again. Observe your fish carefully as they feed. Did every fish get something to eat? If not, at the next feeding increase the amount by just a bit. Small fish may get a slight belly bulge after a good meal, but thicker-bodied fish will not show their full stomachs. If all the food was rapidly eaten, give the same amount at the next feeding. You can gradually increase the amount if you feel you are underfeeding, but it is much better to err on the side of caution. With practice and careful observation you will learn how much food your fish require.

## Snacks Provided By Live Rock

One of the reasons live rock is recommended for any marine tank is that it provides numerous grazing opportunities. The tiny animals that populate live rock offer snacks to your fish, and the algae that grow on it can feed the herbivores in your tank. Such foods rarely are sufficient, and in most fish-only setups they offer little more than a supplement, but it helps. Keep in mind that many reef systems are hardly fed at all. Only a few small fish are included, and the massive invertebrate population in the rock and sandbed provide much of the food they need. The superb control many reef aquarists exercise over the water conditions requires extremely small additions of fish foods. You will certainly be feeding considerably more, but the reef tank situation illustrates that successful aquariums are better served with underfeeding than with overfeeding.

## Improper Diet

Not only do a fish's health and vitality depend on its diet, in many cases its color does too. Faded appearance,

SMALL FRY

### Guaranteed Overfeeding

Children must never be allowed access to fish food. It is hard enough for adults to realize just how little food is needed; children are guaranteed to overfeed. Older kids can feed the fish, but only with direct supervision.

disease, and loss of energy can all be symptoms of an improper diet. A diet lacking in certain nutrients or with those nutrients in the wrong proportions can be considered inadequate or improper. For marine fish such deficiencies are generally traceable to either terrestrial or freshwater ingredients as opposed to marine ingredients, or to a lack of sufficient algae in the diet. This latter applies even to carnivorous fishes.

A coral reef receives so much intense sunlight that an enormous amount of algae grows. There is, however, almost no visible algal growth on the typical reef. This is because of the vast number of herbivorous fishes and invertebrates that are constantly grazing away at the algae. And, it is these fishes and invertebrates that are in turn eaten by carnivores, who benefit from the algae in this second-hand way. Any prepared food that you feed your fishes should have significant amounts of marine algae in it.

To avoid other deficiencies, use foods that contain marine ingredients such as krill, kelp, squid, clams, and shrimp rather than corn, wheat, poultry byproducts, and spinach. Marine ingredients include the fatty acids and other nutrients needed by marine species that are not found in other food sources.

## Hunger Strike

It is certainly possible to spoil your fish, feeding them a preferred food item so much that they begin to refuse any other food. Usually it is just as easy to cure them—just stop feeding the favorite food until they get hungry enough to take other items. Much more

*Research will tell you what your fish should be eating. Improper diets can lead to faded-looking and sick fish.*

serious is when a fish refuses all food, as this signals a dangerous problem. This is why you want to see a fish eat before you buy it. It is very important to get a newly acquired fish eating as soon as possible. If you've seen it eat in the store, you know that there is at least some food that it will accept. It might take a day or two after you bring it home to settle down enough to eat that same food, but you already know it recognizes it as food.

## Cyanide Starvation

One feeding problem is not the fault of the aquarist or of the fish. Animals that have been captured with cyanide often will eat heartily, but no matter how optimal the diet, they waste away and die. It is believed that the digestive system of these fish is irreversibly damaged and that they cannot obtain the nourishment they need regardless of how much they eat. It pays to know the source of the fish you purchase, and it's worth paying a little more for fish from more reliable areas.

## HLLE

Head and lateral line erosion is often seen in captive marines. The causes and treatments are topics of controversy, but the symptoms are straightforward: the sensory pores on the head and the pores of the lateral line become enlarged, then erode. In acute cases there is a major loss of

## Vitamin C

There is a growing body of evidence that vitamin C is important for fish. Unfortunately, vitamin C is fragile and even if it survives processing, it quickly breaks down during storage. Fortunately, many fish foods are available with stabilized vitamin C supplementation. Many hobbyists have found that such foods promote good health in their fish, and they have been used in successful treatment of HLLE.

63

tissue. Many people suspect a pathogen, and bacteria are often cultured from the lesions, but it is not clear whether this represents secondary infection. We include a discussion of HLLE in this chapter on feeding because there is strong evidence of a link to poor diet, at least in some cases. Vitamin C supplementation and feeding plenty of macroalgae are both used in treatment, usually with considerable success. Even more importantly, they appear to be the best preventatives. Fish kept in clean water and fed the proper diet do not develop HLLE.

# Chapter 6

# The World of

# Marine
# Fishes

The availability of fish for the marine hobby is not the same as it is for the freshwater hobby. You may already have noticed that marine fishes tend to be more expensive, but there are other ways that they differ also.

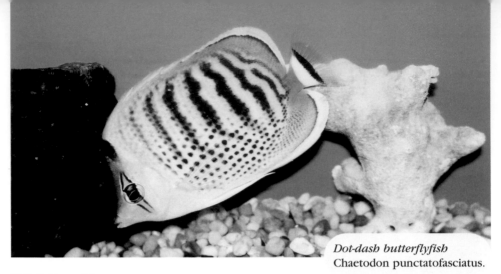

*Dot-dash butterflyfish*
Chaetodon punctatofasciatus.

## Wild-Caught

Let's look first at wild-caught fish. There is a group of freshwater fish whose prices are much more marine-like: the African Rift Lake cichlids. It is no coincidence that these fish also live on reefs, though in this case it is reefs of rock in equatorial lakes, not coral reefs in equatorial seas. Reef fish for the most part must be caught by divers using hand nets. This contrasts with many other species of freshwater aquarium fish, which are netted with seines. Instead of pursuing a single fish in and out of rocky crevices, the fishermen take a net, stretch it across a stream, and pull it in, catching sometimes hundreds of specimens in a dozen or more species. This simply is not possible with coral reef fish in most cases.

The indigenous peoples who typically collect ornamental fish make very little money, receiving only the tiniest fraction of the retail price for each fish. It is therefore not surprising that they will do whatever they can to maximize profits. For a long time the Southeast Asians who collect marine fish used poisons like cyanide to immobilize specimens for netting. The dosage used was sub-lethal, but almost all fish caught with cyanide will eventually die from the poison within weeks after their capture. Cyanide also destroys the reef, killing fish and invertebrates against which it was not intentionally aimed. This all led to the banning of cyanide in capturing ornamental fishes, but the procedure is still performed in remote areas, especially in the Philippines and Indonesia.

The most reasonable solution to such problems is to empower the local people who try to make a living harvesting marine ornamentals. When they are simply dumping the fish off at an exporter and collecting a few cents each, they have little incentive to worry about how their actions affect either the fish or the reef. If on the other hand they have a real stake in the trade and are educated in responsible harvest techniques and can make a living wage using them, then these people can make a major difference. There are groups doing this at various levels.

Some wholesalers are setting up their own collecting stations and educating their employees. Because they can sell directly to the exporter, and because the exporter is also the wholesale distributor, the fishermen can make much more while at the same time protecting the resources of the reef. There is also the Marine Aquarium Council (MAC), a nonprofit organization that supervises the trade in marine ornamentals from the reef to the retailer. Buying fish from MAC-certified stores assures you of superior livestock that was collected with sustainable methods and that brought the local fishermen a reasonable profit at minimal peril. (Learn more at www.aquariumcouncil.org.)

## Commercially Raised

The first successful hobbyist spawnings of freshwater aquarium fish in the United States took place in the 19th Century, and since the mid 20th many species have been raised commercially in farms in Florida and Southeast Asia. Marine fishes, on the other hand, have only recently been spawned and raised for the first time, and commercial production of the first species—gobies, clownfish, dottybacks—has only been in the last couple of decades. More species are being added to the list, including various angelfish. In all cases captive-raised fish are preferable to wild-caught.

*Spotted hawkfish*
Cirrhitichthys aprinus.

## Scientific Names

In this book we rely on scientific names. This may seem to run counter to our simplified approach, but it is not. Common names have no reliability. Aside from the fact that there are no official common names—which means people can (and do) use them as they wish—many marine fish share a common name, and many fish have several common names. On the other hand, almost every fish you'll run into has a unique scientific name (only those too new to science to have been named yet won't have one), and using scientific names is the only way you can be sure about the identity of a fish.

Commercial breeding of marine fish takes place chiefly in North America and Europe, where people tend to be paid a meaningful wage. Many wild-caught marine fish come from Southeast Asia, where people are often paid slave wages. This translates into slightly higher prices for most captive-bred marines than for wild-caught. So why should you buy tank-bred fish? The reason is that their higher price is more than offset by the advantages they provide; they are worth much more than they cost.

These fish do not have to acclimate to captive conditions—they grew up in aquariums! They are very hardy and adapt quickly to their new surroundings. They are not as skittish as wild imports often are. They will eat a wide variety of prepared foods, eagerly gobbling up flake foods that their wild-caught brethren ignore as flotsam. They are also generally free from disease and parasites as well. As an added bonus, they are not taken from the reef, so there is no ecological impact at all from their purchase.

## Aggression Issues

One of the great disappointments of aquarists who come into the hobby through diving on coral reefs is that many of the species of fish that are seen in huge aggregations in the wild cannot be kept in groups in the aquarium. In fact, there are a large number of species for which the standard instruction is *keep only one specimen per aquarium*.

The frustration only grows when aggressive tendencies prevent you from keeping a fish with other members of its genus, or with similar-looking fishes. For example, many of the dwarf angelfish in the genus *Centropyge* make excellent aquarium specimens, but in most cases trying to keep more than one specimen in a tank will lead to violence. In systems larger than 100 gallons (400 liters) it is sometimes possible to keep a small group of one species consisting of one male and two or three females, but otherwise it has to be one per tank.

Copperband
*butterflyfish*
Chelmon rostratus.

Aquarists are constantly trying to overcome this limitation, and those who succeed are often the ones who wind up able to breed these species, since being able to keep a pair in a tank is the first hurdle to overcome. The vast majority, however, just wind up losing fish. In the following descriptions of candidates for your first tank, we will assume that for any given species you can consider only one specimen, and you cannot combine that specimen with fish of any other species in the same genus. Exceptions will be noted.

## Stocking

Most aquarists overstock their tanks. This is a natural consequence of the enthusiasm people have for their hobby; there is never enough tank space for all the fish someone wants. There are a variety of factors that can mitigate the problems caused by overcrowding, and experienced aquarists have learned to manipulate them to minimize tragedies. Unfortunately, two of the factors that define the tanks most likely to be dangerously overstocked are being a marine setup and having a beginning aquarist caring for it. Learning how to assess your system for stocking purposes is one of the most important tasks you can master, but it is also extraordinarily difficult to explain how to acquire this skill.

## Inches per Gallon?

You may come across rules of thumb for stocking an aquarium that specify a certain number of fish inches per gallon, or per square foot of surface area. These "rules" are dangerous in the extreme, since they fail to take into account a host of factors, both biological and physical. While swimming space does figure into

A school of blue-green damselfish Chromis viridis.

stocking concerns, for the most part what is significant is fish flesh— the biomass of the inhabitants of the tank in terms of their needs for oxygen and for waste dilution.

The idea that a 2-inch (5-cm) goby and a 2-inch (5-cm) butterflyfish are in any way equivalent in terms of the demands they place on an aquarium system is ludicrous. The slender, tube-shaped goby is benthic, spending most of its time propped up on the sand outside its burrow. It is also fully grown or close to fully grown. The butterflyfish, on the other hand, is a mere baby, rapidly growing. It is also disc-shaped, meaning that each unit of its length translates into much more fish flesh than the same unit of the goby's body does. The butterfly is also an active swimmer, spending most of its time gliding back and forth in the

tank. A pair of gobies could be maintained in a 10-gallon (40-liter) aquarium, but a single butterflyfish should not be kept in anything smaller than 30 gallons (120 liters), and that only if it is soon going to be moved to something larger as it grows.

So where does this leave the beginner? Unfortunately, there is no formula into which you can plug various factors and come up with an accurate stocking plan. That's why those rules of thumb exist in the first place—beginners lack the experience to make the judgment, and they want some guidance. Unfortunately, that guidance often is harmful.

The last section of this chapter is full of stocking recommendations. These still give plenty of latitude for you to include your favorites, but it keeps you within reasonable limits. It also should avoid any compatibility problems, though you should remember that fish are individuals, and they don't read books like this one.

## A Whirlwind Overview of Marine Fishes

Another way in which marine aquarium fish differ from freshwater ones is in the number of families of fish represented in the typical store's offering. A vast majority of the freshwater fish for sale will be found in the families Callichthyidae, Cichlidae, Characidae, Cobitidae, Cyprinidae, Loricariidae, Osphronemidae, and Poeciliidae. Many other families are represented in the trade, but not in great numbers, and all of the bread-and-butter fish you'll find in any store are in these few families.

Marine fish, on the other hand, are found in a greater number of families, just some of which are Acanthuridae, Antennariidae, Apogonidae, Aulostomidae, Balistidae, Batrachoididae, Blenniidae, Chaetodontidae, Cirrhitidae, Clinidae, Eleotridae, Fistulariidae, Gobiesocidae, Gobiidae, Grammistidae, Labridae, Muraenidae, Opistognathidae, Ostraciidae, Pomacanthidae, Pomacentridae, Sciaenidae, Serranidae, Syngnathidae, and Tetraodontidae.

For the hobbyist, this translates into an enormous variety of fish, with greatly varying needs and habits. Some of these families are themselves huge, containing hundreds if not thousands of species, with considerable variation among them. We obviously can only skim the surface here, but we'll introduce a cross-section of commonly available fish that are suitable for you to consider for your first marine aquarium. It is very important that you research any fish before buying it to check on its needs, its maximize size, and its compatibility with other fish.

*A clownfish and its host anemone.*

## Damsels, including Chromis and Clowns

This group (family Pomacentridae) contains some ideal beginner's fish. They are generally small, hardy, inexpensive, and colorful. Some are extraordinarily aggressive, and a few get really large, but we've sifted those out of the following recommendations.

### Chromis

There are two readily available chromis species worth your attention: *Chromis cyanea* and *C. viridis*. Both are sometimes called the blue chromis, and the latter is also called the green chromis and the blue-green chromis. As this common name situation implies, the first is a vivid blue fish, while the other is a green fish that can appear blue in the right light—as they swim, they appear to be constantly changing color as light reflects off their scales at different angles. These damsels are the exception in that they can be kept in groups. In fact, they are schooling fish and happiest with other members of their species. They are peaceful and hardy and reach about 3 inches (7.5 cm) in length. A less commonly available fish is *C. retrofasciata*, which barely makes 2 inches (4 cm). This is another peaceful schooling species.

### Clowns

Clownfish are well known even outside the aquarium hobby. Also famous is the symbiosis between clownfish and anemones. Anemones, however, can be recommended for only the most advanced hobbyists, and certainly not for a first marine aquarium. Fortunately, although clownfish cannot survive without a host anemone in the wild, they can thrive in an aquarium without one. In fact, generation after generation of clownfish have been raised in commercial breeding establishments without ever seeing an anemone. And that brings up the fact that almost all species of clownfish are available as captive-bred specimens. It will not be hard to find tank-bred clowns for your aquarium, leaving no reason to purchase wild-caught specimens.

What about more than one? In the wild a "family" of clownfish will live together in an anemone. They all arrive at the same time as tiny fish. The dominant fish in the group will become a female and grow to full size. The second most dominant will

## Start with Damsels?

Damsels are highly touted as beginners' fish. Their color and hardiness certainly would suggest that they are, but their feistiness more than compensates for any positive attributes. They are so aggressive and territorial that they can wreak havoc even in a tank of much larger fish—they have been known to attack divers on the reef!

A percula clown showing coloration intermediate between the normal orange and white pattern and the variant black and white pattern.

The World of Marine Fishes

become a functional male and grow to a smaller size. The rest (usually one to three individuals) will remain juveniles. Unless and until one of the pair dies, these juveniles will be non-reproductive and tiny for their entire lives. (This is another reason not to buy wild-caught clownfish—a small specimen might be 10 years old!) If the female is removed, the male will quickly change into a female, and the dominant fish among the juveniles will become the male.

The same scenario can take place in an aquarium without an anemone, but it is best not to push your luck. Stick to two fish only. They should both be very small, guaranteeing they are not yet sexually differentiated, and they will become a mated pair. Whether or not they ever spawn, they should live together peacefully.

The hands-down clownfish for your first tank are the percula clowns, either *Amphiprion ocellaris* or *A. percula*. These orange and white species are so similar it is difficult to tell them apart. You will often come across names like "true percula clown" and "false percula clown," but you should ignore this silliness, and either species will be fine. Also available is a variety in which the orange is replaced with black, making a black and white fish.

## Damsels

The rest of the damsels include some candidates, but also a lot of poor choices. Buying a domino damsel, *Dascyllus trimaculatus,* and then regretting it is almost a rite of passage for marine aquarists, but you can avoid the regret by staying clear of this undeniably appealing little coal-black fish with white polka dots. It will quickly take over your tank, and then it will grow…and grow. It will become a 5-inch (12-cm) monster with faded gray coloration and a nasty attitude.

Aggressive damsels can be included in communities of larger aggressive fish, but not in general community tanks. Fortunately, a blue damsel with a yellow tail, *Chrysiptera parasema,* is more peaceful than most of its relatives and can be kept in many communities without terrorizing all its tankmates. It grows to about 2$^1$/$_2$ inches (7 cm). This species can often be kept in pairs. Do not include it with very passive fish like firefish or shrimp gobies.

## Gobies

Gobies are a gigantic group (about 2,000 species) with worldwide distribution. There are freshwater and brackish species, but most are marine. Most are small, peaceful bottom dwellers that make good aquarium specimens. Notice I did not say that all gobies make good aquarium specimens. You want to be careful about finding the exact species we discuss here or researching any others you come across. There are many small gobies that will work well in your tank,

### A No-Go Goby

The beautiful Catalina goby, *Lythrypnus dalli,* is widely available—unfortunately. This species will not last long in a tropical marine aquarium. Its ideal temperature range is from the mid 60s to the low 70s (18° to 22°C). Even many room temperature setups are too warm for it, and the species will do best in a chilled system.

and we are able to list only a tiny fraction of them.

### Neon Gobies

Neon gobies are almost mandatory in a first marine tank. They are perfect! They're small, colorful, hardy, and peaceful. They also will get along with each other, at least as pairs, though you should be able to keep a half dozen in your tank with plenty of live rock. There are several species referred to as "neon" in the genus *Elacatinus*. The most common is *E. oceanops,* though several other species are found in the trade, such as *E. evelynae* and *E. figaro.* They range in size from about 1$^1$/$_2$ inches (4 cm) to 2 inches (5 cm). Most will act as cleaners, but they will readily accept almost all food offerings. These were among the first marine fish bred in captivity, and they are being produced commercially. Hybrids of various species are also being captive bred; some of them are quite colorful. The only drawback to these fish is their short life span, usually less than two years.

## Clown Gobies

The genus *Gobiodon* has several species well represented in the hobby. The largest, the popular bright yellow *G. citrinus*, is only about 2½ inches (6 cm). They are also called coral gobies because of their association with stony corals. A pair will set up house in a coral head. If a small group is kept together, they should pair up. These tadpole-shaped fish are spunky and full of personality, and their poisonous slime keeps them safe from most predators. They cannot, however, compete with aggressive feeders. So they need to be part of a live-and-let-live community.

## Shrimp/Prawn/Watchman Gobies

Shrimp gobies pair up with shrimp. The basically blind shrimp digs and maintains a burrow and keeps an antenna on the goby at all times. When the goby sees danger, they both zip into the burrow. Many fish in the genera *Amblyeleotris* and *Cryptocentrus* are between 3 and 6 inches (7 and 15 cm) and make good aquarium specimens. Another genus of gobies is *Stonogobiops*, which are

*Yellownose prawn goby* Stonogobiops xanthorhinica.

small and very colorful. If you can get them, alpheid shrimp will often pair up with these gobies in an aquarium.

## Firefish

Firefish, also known as dartfish or dart gobies, hang in the water waiting for tidbits to drift by. The first sign of potential danger sends them darting into an awaiting burrow. These fish in the genus *Nemateleotris* can make fine aquarium specimens, but they absolutely cannot compete with aggressive fish or active feeders. Best for your first tank is *N. magnifica*. They are usually tolerant of conspecifics, but in a tank the size that our protocol

*Pajama cardinalfish*
Sphaeramia nematoptera.

specifies, you should probably keep a maximum of two.

## Blennies

Blennies are another large and diverse group of fishes, many of them suitable for the aquarium. Once again, it is vital that you research any blenny before purchasing it. Some are very aggressive and some are very large, but many are great for your tank.

The lawnmower blenny, *Salarias fasciatus,* is popular because of its great appetite for hair algae. Reaching about 5¹/₂ inches (14 cm), this fish needs a diet of algae, whether growing naturally or supplemented by the aquarist. It is generally peaceful with other fish, but should be kept one per tank.

The bicolor blenny, *Ecsenius bicolor,* is about 4 inches (10 cm) long. It is a colorful, captivating specimen. Aquarists disagree on its aggressiveness toward other members of the species, but most agree that it is

peaceful with other fish.

The beautiful gold and lavender Midas or Persian blenny, *Ecsenius midas,* reaches 5 inches (13 cm) and is generally safe with all but the most passive fish but should be kept only one per tank. Unlike many other popular blennies, this species is a carnivore and requires meaty foods.

Fang blennies of the genus *Meiacanthus* have venomous fangs usually used only in defense. Some are being bred commercially. They vary greatly in their peacefulness, and you should research a particular species before purchase.

## Cardinal Fish

Cardinal fish are also excellent aquarium candidates. They are fairly small and very peaceful. They actually enjoy being kept in small groups and tolerate their own kind very well. They have large eyes and are most comfortable when they can retire to a dark hole or under a ledge to get out of bright light.

*Lawnmower blenny*
Salarias fasciatus.

A feature that sets this group apart from almost all other marine species is that they are mouthbrooders, and their fry are not planktonic. The male incubates the large eggs in his mouth, and when he releases the fry they are miniatures of the adults and able to eat foods like baby brine shrimp. This makes breeding these fish a real possibility, even for a beginning aquarist. There are several species common in the hobby.

*Pterapogon kauderni*, sometimes called the Banggai cardinal, is striking with its silver and black coloration. Its unusual body shape adds to its appeal. Although only recently introduced to the hobby, it was an instant favorite. It has suffered severe population decline in the wild, so you should only buy tank-bred specimens. This species is a little feistier than other cardinals. If you can get a male-female pair, that should work; otherwise stick to one in the tank.

The similar *Sphaeramia nematoptera* and *S. orbicularis* are commonly available and always popular with their unusual shape and coloration. They stay under 4 inches (10 cm).

The genus *Apogon* has many suitable species, some of which are usually available. Several have the red coloration that gave this group their common name of cardinal, and many have vivid horizontal striping.

## Dwarf Angelfish

Angelfish are generally unsuitable for your tank, mainly because they grow too large. Many of the dwarf angels, however, are good candidates. These angelfish in the genus *Centropyge* have mixed reputations. They are simultaneously known as hardy and hard-to-keep; they are considered by some people to be safe in a reef tank, while others claim they will eat corals and other ornamental invertebrates. Some of this discrepancy is due to differences from one species to another, some is due to individual differences, and some is simply circumstantial—the same fish in a different context would behave differently.

A single dwarf angel is a possibility for your tank, but only

*Pygmy angelfish* Centropyge argi.

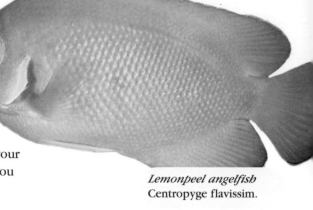

*Lemonpeel angelfish*
Centropyge flavissim.

later in the game. If you want to include one, leave room for it when you stock your tank. After three or four months, when the tank is maturing and you have some experience, you can purchase the angel and put it in your quarantine tank. Six weeks later you can introduce it into your main aquarium.

The pygmy angel, *Centropyge argi,* is about 3 inches (8 cm), while the popular lemonpeel angel, *C. flavissima,* reaches twice that length. One of the most sought-after species is the flame angel, *C. loricula,* which is hardy and colorful. If you want to include a dwarf angel in your aquarium, make sure to leave room by stocking the tank very lightly.

## Tangs

Fish known as tangs or surgeonfish are among the most sought-after marines. Especially common in the hobby are the blue and black *Paracanthurus hepatus* and the yellow *Zebrasoma flavescens.* Aside from their grace and beauty, most species of tangs are dedicated algae eaters and will help keep a tank algae free. The tank in this protocol is barely large enough to house a single tang of the smaller species, and even then not at first.

Tangs usually get along with all tankmates except for other tangs, but they are not very disease-hardy. Like dwarf angels, tangs should only be acquired after you have

Saltwater Aquariums

## Dwarf Angels Only

Large marine angelfish are among the most beautiful of all fish. Their regal bearing and beautiful colors capture the attention of all who view them. While some are nearly impossible to keep in captivity, several species are hardy to the extreme. The juvenile and adult colorations differ greatly, and babies are readily available in the trade. These fish, however, are simply too large. The smaller species require tanks of 100 gallons (400 liters) or more, while the larger ones reach lengths of 2 feet (60 cm) and require 200-gallon (750-liter) or bigger aquariums. You must stick with the dwarf species.

## Fish To Avoid

Two fish have no place in your tank, despite the fact that they are inexpensive, small, peaceful, and very colorful.

First is a cleaner wrasse of the genus *Labroides*. These fish can survive only by eating parasites and bits of flesh off larger fish. They will starve to death in the aquarium, since it takes a reef full of fish to feed the relatively few cleaners found there.

Second is a mandarin; the mandarins are also known as dragonets or dragon gobies. Mandarins are in the genus *Synchiropus* and come in a variety of colors. These highly appealing fish will not survive in your tank, because they require a steady diet of copepod crustaceans. No matter how much you want one, resist. These fish can be kept successfully, but only in very large—like 200-gallon (750-liter)—aquariums that are mature reef setups with no other copepod predators in them. If you go on in the marine hobby, you may someday be able to keep a mandarin, but not now.

experience, and they should only be put into mature tanks. It is vitally important to include macroalgae (seaweed) in their diet; many aquarists use the dried seaweed sold as sushi wrapping. A tang needs strict quarantine, and you should definitely have some cleaners as tankmates when it comes out of quarantine. The best tang to try after you have experience is the yellow tang, *Zebrasoma flavescens*. It is a beautiful solid yellow, and although it does reach about 8 inches (20 cm), this is not too large for your tank, provided it is not overstocked.

## Triggers and Puffers

The order Tetraodontiformes includes two popular families, the triggerfish, Balistidae, and the puffers, Tetraodontidae. These fish are hearty, hardy, and fascinating. Many actually become pets, interacting with their owners and even enjoying an occasional pat on the back. Unfortunately, they are generally unsuitable for your first aquarium. Almost all of the species in these two families are too large for your tank, and too aggressive. Triggerfish especially are noted for sudden and unprovoked violence, often killing every other fish in the tank. They may also bite the hand that feeds them, and they have sharp teeth and strong jaws!

It is, however, possible for a beginning marine aquarist to have one of these personable fish, but it usually requires a larger aquarium than in our protocol. There are a few possibilities for a special application of our

*Royal gramma*
Gramma loreto.

protocol—the specimen tank. In such a setup, the tank houses only one fish. The section on stocking schemes found at the end of this chapter will give more information.

## Basslets

Technically, marine basses are fish in the family Serranidae, but in practice both "bass" and "basslet" are extremely loosely defined. For example, the freshwater "largemouth bass" is actually in the family Centrarchidae, which also includes the sunfish. The fish sold under the names bass and basslets in the aquarium trade are often in the family Serranidae, but not always. Many include grammas and dottybacks as well. In this section we will treat all of these groups, regardless of actual taxonomy. Because of the enormous variation in size and behavior among all the fishes in this group, it is especially important that you check out any potential purchases, especially for mature size—many basses will quickly outgrow your aquarium.

The chalk basslet, *Serranus tortugarum,* grows to a bit over 3

inches (8 cm) and is an ideal fish for the beginning aquarist. It is small, colorful, and generally peaceful. Although it can be kept in small groups in larger tanks (over 100 gallons/400 liters), you should stick with one.

The lantern bass, *Serranus baldwini,* is another great choice. It is good for communities with species that can stand up to a little aggression.

The royal gramma, *Gramma loreto,* is a perennial favorite, purple in front and bright yellow in back. It minds its own business, for the most part, but will not tolerate any other fish of similar shape or color in the tank. It reaches a maximum of 3 inches (8 cm). The related blackcap basslet, *Gramma melacara,* also is a beauty, combining rich purple, black, and

*Yellowhead jawfish*
Opistognathus aurifrons.

white. It grows about an inch larger than the royal gramma.

At first glance, dottybacks are ideal fish. They are hardy, small, extremely colorful, and available as tank-bred fish. What's the catch? They are absolute monsters, territorial to the extreme and willing to take on fish much larger than they are. The least aggressive is the orchid dottyback, *Pseudochromis fridmani*, and while "least aggressive dottyback" does not mean it isn't aggressive, it can be kept with tough tankmates. You cannot keep more than one dottyback of any kind in a tank, nor can you include similarly shaped or colored fish like grammas.

## Jawfish

Several jawfish, genus *Opistognathus*, make interesting aquarium specimens, but you can't go wrong with *O. aurifrons*, known as the pearly or yellow-headed jawfish. They get about 4 inches (10 cm) long, but most of the time you will just see their heads sticking out of the sand. They require a fairly deep sandbed in which to dig their vertical burrows. You can keep more than one in a tank.

## Wrasses

The wrasses of the family Labridae are another huge and diverse group with interesting body shapes and coloration, ranging in size from truly small to gargantuan. The latter is well represented by the Napoleon or humphead wrasse, *Cheilinus undulatus*, with reported lengths up to $7^1/_2$ feet (2.3 m) and weights of 420 pounds (190 kg). Unfortunately, you may find juveniles of this particular species for sale as aquarium specimens! The other end of the spectrum, however, includes many small- to medium-size wrasses that make colorful, active, and interesting aquarium residents. Many of these small species are called fairy or flasher wrasses; these brightly patterned, active fish will liven up any aquarium. Many wrasses will eat motile invertebrates such as sandbed animals and even algae-eating snails, hermit crabs, and shrimp. They are all heavy, eager, greedy feeders, so they are not good tankmates for meek species.

The six-line wrasse, *Pseudocheilinus hexataenia*, and others in its genus are excellent choices for an aquarium, but they can be quite aggressive and do not usually tolerate conspecifics in their tank.

Flasher wrasses of the genus *Paracheilinus* are quite peaceful, and they can usually be kept in small groups as long as there is not more than one male. If you buy small

81

The World of Marine Fishes

## Wrasse ID

Before purchasing a wrasse for your aquarium, make sure you research the species to make sure it does not get too large and is not too aggressive.

specimens, only one male should develop as they mature.

## Hawkfish

Hawkfish get their name from their habit of perching on a rock or coral until they detect a prey animal moving below them, at which point they swoop down and snap it up. Several species are good aquarium candidates, but the best is probably the longnose hawkfish, *Oxycirrhites typus*, which reaches about 5 inches (13 cm). You can have only one hawkfish of any kind per tank, and you cannot keep it with any fish, worm, shrimp, or crab that is small enough for it to eat.

## Butterflies

Almost all butterflyfish are not suitable for our protocol. The exceptions are, however, fantastic choices—the bannerfish or banner butterflies of the genus *Heniochus*. The only concern is their size, as they get large but are happiest when not alone. Two is the maximum number for this protocol's tank. There are several species that are imported, but the most common is *H. acuminatus*. These fish are very hardy and will usually accept all types of food.

## Frogfish

Most people would not recommend frogfish or any of their relatives to the beginning aquarist. The major reasons

*Warty frogfish*
Antennarius maculatus.

deal with their voracious appetites and cavernous maws. Several species are small enough for your tank. The commonly available *Antennarius maculatus* reaches only about 6 inches (15 cm), so it can be kept in a tank of the size our protocol calls for. If you are willing to undertake the special care this species will require, you can certainly keep one as a pet in the aquarium by itself. See the stocking section at the end of this chapter for details.

## Seahorses

Despite their near-universal appeal, seahorses are very poor candidates for your first marine tank. The arrival in the market of captive-bred strains of various seahorse species, however, makes them a possible avenue of specialization for you six months or a year down the road. Get some experience before trying these fantastic but challenging animals that require a tank unto themselves as well as special feeding.

## Moray

A moray eel? Yes, there is one you can keep as a single specimen: *Echidna nebulosa*, the snowflake moray. A 50-gallon (200-liter) aquarium is the smallest you can use for one of these eels, and when it reaches its full 3 feet (1 meter) of length you might want to get a larger tank, especially if you want to keep it with other fish.

Other fish, with a moray eel? Yes, this moray is a crustacean and mollusk

### Show Restraint

We all have to fight the impulse to purchase every fascinating and colorful fish in our dealer's tanks, but for children it is especially difficult to pass on a favored specimen. Explaining that a certain fish gets too big for your tank or would be nasty toward the other fish in it can help them realize that these are individual animals with specific traits, not just animate ornaments.

eater. It has flat, crushing teeth to deal with its prey's shells. It cannot be trusted with small fish it can swallow whole, but it will not actively hunt down and chew up other fish. Of course, to keep it with a few larger fish, you will need a larger aquarium than when keeping it by itself.

## Invertebrates

Many marine tanks contain small snails and small hermit crabs as scavengers and algae eaters. Sometimes people add tiny burrowing starfish to their sandbeds as well. These critters crawl around and clean up, including in the nooks and crannies among the live

*Predatory fish will eat snails and hermit crabs. Stock your tank minus the former if you want to enjoy the latter.*

groups, many need the same one-per-tank rule as many fish have. Large shrimp will often eat smaller species.

The advice to do your homework applies here as well. For example, while many snails make great cleanup critters, some are predatory and will eat other snails. In fact, except for the small herbivorous snails common in the hobby, you should avoid all other mollusks, including scallops, clams, octopuses, etc. The beautiful tridacnid clams (giant clams) at your retailer's require the most exacting conditions in a reef tank and cannot be included in this protocol in any way.

## Suggested Stocking Schemes

By picking one of the schemes listed below you will avoid untold problems with your first marine aquarium. You must realize that these are not intended to be mix-and-match. Each community should work very well by itself, but there is no general substitutability among them. Many types of fish appear in more than one stocking, so if you have a particular favorite you should be able to find several choices that include it. In addition, there are choices in each stocking scheme, with, for example, the listing of one specimen chosen from a list of several to fill one slot. You can swap out similar fish, for example a goby for a similar blenny, but do so only in conjunction with research into the traits of each.

rock. They are useful additions to your tank, but only if you are not housing any predatory fish like hawkfish or wrasses. If you have such fish, the snails and hermits will become expensive fish food!

Other invertebrates are also appropriate for some setups. Shrimp, starfish, crabs, and lobsters can make interesting aquarium inhabitants. There is always a balance that must be struck between predatory fish and predatory invertebrates. Either might consume the other, so you must take into account the relative sizes and normal diet of any animals you want to combine in one aquarium. Many crustaceans are highly cannibalistic, and while some shrimp will live in

## Concentrating on Small Fish

When you stick with small fish, you can have quite a variety in your aquarium. With only small specimens, you can really get the sense of an expansive reef, with more than a dozen fish flitting about the piles of live rock.

6 chromis, either *Chromis viridis* or *C. cyanea*

4 neon gobies, *Elactinus* spp.

2 clown gobies, *Gobiodon* spp.

1 royal gramma, *Gramma loreto*

1 peaceful *Meiacanthus* goby

6 peppermint shrimp, *Lysmata wurdemanni*

## A Typical Community #1

Most marine communities contain a wide assortment of fish. Here is one that should work nicely.

1 damsel

2 clowns, *Amphiprion ocellatus* or *A. percula*

1 chalk basslet, *Serranus tortugarum*

1 flasher wrasse *Paracheilinus*

3 cardinalfish, all the same species

1 coral banded shrimp, *Stenopus hispidus*, or a mated pair

## A Typical Community #2

Here is another colorful community.

1 lantern bass, *Serranus baldwini*

1 dottyback, *Pseudochromis fridmani*

1 Banggai cardinal, *Pterapogon kauderni*

1 yellow hogfish, *Bodianus bimaculatus*

2 flasher wrasses, *Paracheilinus* sp.

1 Midas blenny, *Ecsenius midas*

## A Peaceful Community

The following are all passive fish that do not fare well with aggressive feeders.

2 firefish

3 clown gobies

4 neon gobies

2 jawfish

6 peppermint shrimp, *Lysmata wurdemanni*

## Centered on a Tang

This tank will be sparsely populated at first to leave room for a yellow tang to be added after six months to a year.

2 damsels

1 small wrasse

1 basslet

(1 yellow tang, *Zebrasoma flavescens*)

*Yellow tang*
Zebrasoma flavescens.

## Larger Fish

A smaller number of larger fish can make a wonderful community as well. It is a waste of money to buy hermit crabs, snails, or live sand critters with these predators, as they will quickly consume all of them.

1 six-line wrasse, *Pseudocheilinus hexataenia*

1 longnose hawkfish, *Oxycirrhites typus*

1 lawnmower blenny, *Salarias fasciatus*

1 bicolor goatfish, *Parupeneus barberinoides*

## Place for an Angel

In this community we reserve space for a dwarf angelfish to be added after six months to a year.

1 bicolor blenny, *Ecsenius bicolor*

1 hawkfish

1 orchid dottyback, *Pseudochromis fridmani*

1 yellow wrasse *Halichoeres chrysus*

(1 *Centropyge* angel)

## Specimen Tank: Frogfish

If a tank containing a single fish that blends in with its background and hardly ever moves appeals to you, you can keep the frogfish *Antennarius maculatus* as a pet. This fish makes up for its shortcomings with fascinating features. Instead of swimming, it typically moves by walking, using its stubby pectoral fins as legs. It also sports a built-in fishing pole and lure, which it wiggles to mimic a small fish, enticing fish to come close enough to be inhaled in a gulp that is one of the fastest movements of all animals. Since it can eat fish almost as large as itself, this frogfish is an obvious candidate for a one-specimen display.

## Specimen Tank: Moray Eel

You can keep a snowflake moray eel, *Echidna nebulosa*, under our protocol,

*Snowflake moray eel*
Echidna nebulosa.

Valentinni's sharpnose pufferfish
Canthigaster valentini.

but the shorter, wider 50-gallon tank is preferable to the narrower, taller 55, since the greater bottom area is better for this bottom-dweller. Build your live rock to provide several caves for the fish. Feed it bits of fish or shellfish, and keep up with your water changes. It is a good idea to feed two or three times a week, performing a water change a day after each feeding.

## Specimen Tank: Butterflies

You can keep two bannerfish, *Heniochus* sp. The size of your tank limits you to just these two fish, but they will make a grand display. While they are small, you could add a school of six chromis, but only if you are prepared to find another home for them when the bannerfish get larger.

## Specimen Tank: Puffer

Although most puffers get too large for a tank fitting our protocol, there are exceptions. Many puffers in the genus *Canthigaster*, often called tobies, grow to 8 inches (20 cm) or less. A few other puffers stay this small as well. Another candidate is a boxfish such as *Chilomycterus scheopfi*. A single fish of this size can be housed in a tank set up according to our protocol, and two habits of puffers make them ideal for such a system: they rarely get along with other fish, and they often like to interact with their keepers. By itself a puffer will not get into trouble, and it will have plenty of time and attention for that weird creature on the other side of the glass that often comes with treats to eat.

# Chapter 7

# Feeling Good

When it comes to fish health, there is something that you must understand: it is much easier to prevent fish diseases than to treat them. Proper husbandry is the key to keeping your fish healthy. You may have noticed in Chapter 3, when discussing aquarium setup, that no medications were mentioned.  There are several reasons for this, but central to them all is the fact that you cannot medicate your aquarium.

**K**eep in mind that a marine aquarium is chemically complex and that most of its filtration is done by bacteria that are as susceptible to drugs as disease bacteria are. When you factor in the extreme sensitivity of many live rock organisms to the chemicals often used in aquarium medications, you can see that adding drugs to your tank will do more harm than good. And if that isn't enough reason for you, consider that injection is the best way to administer antibiotics to fish and that dumping antibiotics into the tank water seldom has much positive effect. So what do you do? Let's talk about preventing disease first, and then we'll come back to medicating.

## Prevention of Illness

Our protocol calls for a four-step program for disease prevention:

1. Observation
2. Eating
3. Acclimation
4. Quarantine

### Observation

The first step is to carefully inspect any fish before you consider purchasing it. This comes after you get excited about its color,

shape, or behavior and after you have researched to make sure the fish is suitable for your aquarium. It means being as objective as you possibly can and examining it for any sign of injury or illness. What do you look for? Anything unusual—this is where having looked up the fish to see what is normal for the species is important. You don't want to buy a fish that exhibits missing scales, ripped fins, open sores, white spots, black spots, red bruises, uncharacteristic listlessness, uncharacteristic activity, or any other anomaly. It is best to avoid a fish if any of the fish in the same tank exhibit any of these symptoms, even if the one you want appears free of problems.

You need to use some latitude in judgment, of course. A fish that normally lingers in the entrance to its private cave but is being housed in a bare tank will appear flighty and

*If you are giving your fish the attention they need you will notice any changes in their daily routine, good or bad.*

*The water at your dealer may be quite different chemically from your aquarium's water. New purchases must be acclimated carefully to avoid potentially lethal shock.*

frightened. Shy species kept with aggressive ones will be hiding in the corners. Nevertheless, a few minutes spent watching a potential purchase can reveal a lot of things. Patience is important. In fact, if you can, come back in a few days and observe things again. Many problems manifest themselves quickly, so the longer the fish has been in the store, the better. The most important behavior of all to observe is feeding.

## Eating

Our protocol requires that you ask your retailer to show you the fish eating. This accomplishes several things, as we have already noted. There are exceptions, but it often works out that a fish that is not eating will never eat. This may be because of stress, illness, or simple inability to adjust to captivity. You will also want to be able to tell whether the animal you're considering will take prepared foods. If you see it eat live brine shrimp, it's good that it's eating, but seeing it take pellets is even better, since it means that feeding the fish isn't going to be a problem.

## Acclimation

Acclimation refers to preparing a newly acquired fish to move from the water in which it has been transported into the water of its tank. This is another area where there is an enormous variation of opinion and where many customary approaches are seriously flawed. Our protocol calls for drip acclimation.

1. Take out a bucket and your acclimation kit. Secure a plastic or glass bowl of a size that when the transport bag is emptied into it, the fish will still be covered with water.

## A Full Tub

**Before purchasing any fish, make sure that your mixing tub is full of mixed water of the correct temperature to be used when you bring the fish home.**

Set the bowl at the bottom of the bucket, open the bag the fish are in, and gently pour them and all the water into the bowl. (If there is sufficient water in the bag to cover the fish after they've been put into the bucket, you can dispense with the bowl. If not, you can remove the bowl once the level in the bucket is high enough.)

2. Situate the bucket below the level of the tank into which the fish will go, on either the floor or a sturdy chair. Cut the tubing into two pieces and attach one to each side of the valve. Open the valve and submerge the entire device in the tank into which the fish will be going. Maneuver it to get all the air bubbles out. Keeping one end submerged, put your thumb over the other end and lower that end into the bowl. Take your thumb off, and the water should begin flowing into the bowl. Quickly close the valve. Use clothespins to attach both ends of the tubing, one to the tank and the other to the bucket, so that they stay in place.

3. Now open the valve just enough that water drips into the bowl, about five or six drops per second. It will eventually overflow the bowl and begin filling the bucket. The goal is to increase the original volume in the bucket three or four times over the course of two hours.

4. At this point, you can top off the water in the aquarium from pre-mixed water from your mixing tub. Net the fish out and place them into the aquarium. Now discard the water in the bucket. Do not pour it back into the tank.

## Quarantine

Quarantine provides a two-pronged approach to disease prevention. It isolates new fish, which can be carrying disease organisms, from the rest of your fish, giving you time to detect and treat any illnesses. It also provides your new fish, stressed from capture and transport, a safe and peaceful place to recuperate, settle in, and get used to your water conditions before they have to brave the established gang and any microbes to which your current fish are immune but to which your new fish may not be. Quarantine should last at least three weeks to make sure the new fish are not going to be delivering pathogens into your main aquarium. Twice that is preferable.

All purchases must be quarantined for several weeks before adding them

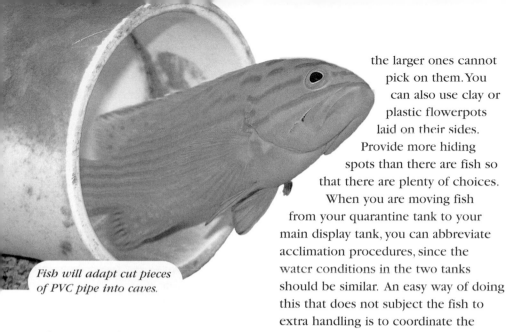

Fish will adapt cut pieces of PVC pipe into caves.

the larger ones cannot pick on them. You can also use clay or plastic flowerpots laid on their sides. Provide more hiding spots than there are fish so that there are plenty of choices. When you are moving fish from your quarantine tank to your main display tank, you can abbreviate acclimation procedures, since the water conditions in the two tanks should be similar. An easy way of doing this that does not subject the fish to extra handling is to coordinate the move with a water change on your main tank. Drain the quarantine tank

to the main tank. It is a good idea to keep the small sponge filter for the quarantine tank running all the time in a back corner of your main tank so that it always has a functioning biofilter.

Your quarantine tank should be set up for a day or two before you go shopping for new fish. While your fish are acclimating, you can move the sponge filter in and furnish the tank. You need to provide hiding places for the new fish. Pieces of PVC pipe of appropriate diameters make excellent "caves." These are especially good if you have fish of different sizes; by supplying pipes of different diameters, the smaller fish can hide away where

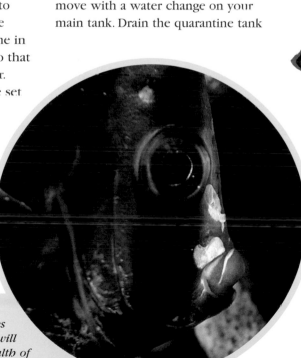

Quarantining new purchases and sick fish will improve the health of all fish in your care.

down so that the fish are just covered with water. Then slowly add water from your main tank until the quarantine tank is full again. You can then net out the fish and place it directly into the main tank. (You should feed the main tank first and turn off the light to minimize aggression against the newcomer.)

## Cleaners

An optional but recommended fifth way of preventing disease is to employ the services of cleaners. Many species of shrimp and gobies will clean fish of parasites and other unwanted tissue. Two of the best are neon gobies and peppermint shrimp. The presence of these animals in an aquarium is often sufficient to forestall outbreaks of parasitic diseases like marine "ich"

*Peppermint shrimp* Lysmata wurdemanni *will serve as cleaners, eating parasites off their fish tankmates.*

(*Cryptocaryon*), since they quickly consume the parasites as soon as they appear. Just remember to purchase cleaner gobies, not cleaner wrasses. These fish will not survive in captivity, and their harvest leaves the reef susceptible to decimation by disease.

## Treatment of Illness

The first rule is that the only place you can treat sick fish is in your quarantine tank. If you follow our protocol for disease prevention, any problems you may encounter will most likely be with new fish that are in quarantine after purchase. However, if a fish in your main tank becomes ill and you feel you must treat it, it should be netted out and placed into the quarantine tank, which can be pressed into duty as a hospital tank. In this case you should fill the quarantine tank with water from the main aquarium in order to avoid any possible stress from different water conditions. Let's take a look at the common ailments you may run into.

## Minor Injuries

Newly acquired fish may arrive with split or frayed fins, missing scales, or bruises. You of course would not select an injured fish, but it can be hurt during netting and transport. Also, fish already in your aquarium may have a run-in with a sharp rock or a territorial tankmate and wind up with similar wounds. Fortunately, fish normally recover spontaneously from such

*Sick fish need to be placed in a quarantine tank and treated immediately.*

injuries. Keep an eye on them in case they become infected, but otherwise just leave them to heal naturally.

## Diseases

The most common diseases of marine fish are parasitic in origin. We humans are more likely to suffer from a bacterial or viral infection; the former respond to antibiotic treatments, and the latter can only be treated with rest and plenty of fluids. While there are bacteria and viruses that attack fish, they are fortunately rarely encountered—fortunately because there is little you can do to treat them.

Parasitic diseases typically feature an organism that spends part of its life cycle attached to a fish, feeding on the fish's tissues, and part of its life cycle elsewhere—free swimming, in the substrate, etc. The organism is often unaffected by medications except at a certain point in the life cycle. The typical scenario is that a parasite

attaches to a host fish and feeds on its fluids and tissues, then after a time drops off and enters a stage during which it rapidly reproduces, typically within a cyst that ruptures, releasing all new parasites that immediately seek out hosts. It is easy to see how these organisms can quickly overwhelm a tank and why daily siphoning of the tank bottom can be effective in removing hundreds, even thousands, of the pests.

There are four parasitic diseases of marine fish that are commonly encountered by hobbyists. All of them attack the body of the fish, especially the gills. As the gills become clogged with mucus and parasites, the fish may gasp for breath. It will also scrape itself against rocks and other surfaces as if it had itches (which it probably does). All four of the parasites are consumed by cleaner shrimp and fish, and, since the host fish will permit the cleaners to enter their mouths and gills, it is

Feeling Good

## Quarantine Length

It is no accident that the recommend quarantine length is four to six weeks. This is the length of time you have to wait to make sure the common disease organisms have completed their life cycles.

possible for cleaners to prevent outbreaks of these diseases. This does not mean you should be sloppy with quarantine procedures, since cleaners cannot be counted on 100 percent, but keeping a few cleaners in your aquarium is good insurance.

Remember that you cannot treat fish in the main aquarium. The first step in treating the fish is a freshwater bath. This causes many of the parasites to fall free of the fish's body and helps it breathe more easily. You can place the fish into a container of fresh water of the same temperature as the water it was in. If it is not showing extreme stress after one minute, let it remain in the bath for another minute. Then move it (back) to the quarantine tank. Gradually lower the salinity in the tank to a specific gravity of about 1.010 (some aquarists go as low as 1.009). Gradually means over the course of two days, removing some water and

replacing it with fresh water until the desired salinity is reached. Known as the hyposalinity treatment, it works because the parasites cannot osmoregulate, meaning they cannot adjust the salt content within their bodies. Since that content is about the same as that of seawater, water enters their cells by osmosis when they are exposed to water of lower salinity, and the cells eventually burst. Fish, on the other hand, can handle this level of salinity quite well. Invertebrates cannot, and they will die if exposed to hyposalinity. The treatments should last a minimum of four weeks, preferably six weeks, to make sure all the parasites have completed their life cycles and have been eradicated.

All of these ailments can be cured just with hyposalinity, especially with daily water changes in which the bottom of the tank is thoroughly vacuumed, removing all parasites resting there, but recovery is more rapid and more certain if this is coupled with chemical treatment. The medicine of choice differs from one disease to another.

If despite quarantine one of these diseases makes its way into your main tank, you have the problem of cleansing the aquarium of the parasites that are in the free-living stages of their life cycles. Removing all fish eliminates the parasites eventually, because they cannot find a host when they need it. In some cases you have to wait several

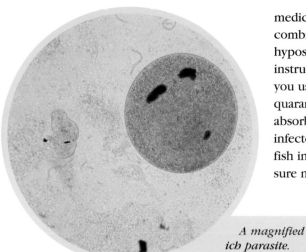

medications, which can be used in combination with freshwater dips and hyposalinity. Follow the manufacturer's instructions carefully, and make sure you use the medication only in a bare quarantine tank, as the chemicals are absorbed by substrates and rocks. An infected tank must be left without any fish in it for at least a month to make sure no parasites are left.

*A magnified ich parasite.*

## Velvet

Also known as oodinium or coral fish disease, velvet is caused by the protozoan *Amyloodinium ocellatum*. By the time tiny white or brownish specks appear on the fins and body with a powdery or velvety appearance, the fish's gills are typically heavily infected.

Copper medications are also effective against velvet and can be used

Feeling Good

months before putting fish back into the tank. This is yet another reason why the use of a quarantine tank is so important, to prevent these organisms from ever getting into your main tank.

## White Spot

The protozoan *Cryptocaryon irritans* causes a disease known as white spot or marine "ich." The latter name derives from the similarity of this malady to the freshwater ailment nicknamed "ich," an abbreviation of the organism's name, *Ichthyophthirius.* Unlike the other three parasitic diseases, this disease usually begins with an apparent salting of the body with white spots, and the parasites later move to the gills. This makes it easier to treat, since you can catch it in the early stages.

The free-swimming stage of the organism is susceptible to copper-based

SMALL FRY

### Be Prepared

One of the bittersweet things about keeping pets is that it can introduce children to the realities of illness and death. It is natural for them to be upset if a fish dies, but this can become a teaching opportunity when handled with compassion.

Do not fall for clever advertising. There are no medications that are safe for use in anything other than a quarantine or hospital aquarium. You must remove a fish to treat it. Of course, with proper quarantine procedure you should not face the problem of a sick fish in your main tank in the first place.

along with freshwater dips and hyposalinity. It takes three to four weeks for a tank without fish to become free of the parasites.

### Black Spot

Black spot or tang disease, also called black ich, is actually caused by very small flatworms in the genus *Paravortex*. It is primarily a disease of tangs or surgeons, though it can affect other species as well. The worms spend only about a week feeding on a fish, appearing as black spots the size of salt grains. The rest of their life cycle is spent burrowing in the substrate.

Unfortunately, the traditional drug of choice is formalin, which has been found to be extraordinarily dangerous and is now strictly regulated. Consult your dealer to find a medication effective against black spot disease. A tank must be left without fish for at least four months before you can reintroduce fish without reinfecting them.

### Brooklynella

Also known as clownfish disease, brooklynella is caused by the parasite *Brooklynella hostilis.* Although primarily an affliction of clownfish and other damsels, it can also affect a wide variety of other species. This protozoan multiplies more quickly than the other three, so it is especially dangerous and deadly. As with velvet, the organism attacks the gills first. A fish infected with brooklynella produces large quantities of body slime.

Treatment for this disease is problematic. Once you can make the diagnosis the fish is already quite ill, and the traditional medication of choice, again formalin, can finish off the patient as well as the disease organisms even if it were legally obtainable. At least with a quarantine tank you can contain the infection, and if the fish dies, you can sterilize the setup with a diluted bleach solution. The fish in your main tank will be saved, even if your new fish cannot be.

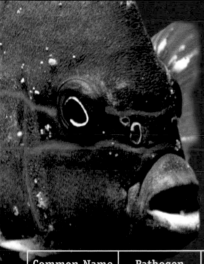

# Common Diseases

| Common Name | Pathogen | Symptoms | Treatment | Life Cycle |
|---|---|---|---|---|
| Ich, white spot | *Cryptocaryon irritans* | White spots on body and fins | Freshwater dip, hyposalinity, proprietary ich medication | One month |
| Velvet, oodinium, coral fish disease | *Amyloodium ocellatum* | Gill infection first, then tiny white or brown specks on body and fins | Freshwater dip, hyposalinity, proprietary velvet medication | Three to four weeks |
| Black spot, tang disease, black ich | *Paravortex* worms | Small black spots on body | Freshwater dip, hyposalinity, proprietary black spot medication | Four to six months |
| Brooklynella, clown fish disease | *Brooklynella hostilis* | Gill infection first, then large quantity of body slime | Freshwater dip, hyposalinity (medicating is problematic) | At least a month |

# Chapter 8

# What's Next?

If you follow the protocol in this book, you should have a thriving marine aquarium, and you will have mastered the knowledge and skills necessary to become a marine aquarist. What's more, you may have discovered one or more aspects of this hobby that you would like to pursue in greater depth. Even if that's not the case, there is no reason you cannot continue to enjoy your saltwater tank for years to come, and this chapter will describe some of the directions you can take if you want to branch out.

## Join a Club

No matter what part of the aquarium hobby interests you, you can benefit greatly from joining a local aquarium society. The fellowship and education you gain will help you enjoy your hobby to the fullest. There are also clubs that specialize in the marine side of the hobby. These clubs can be very helpful to you as a marine aquarist, especially if you are thinking of starting a reef tank.

Aside from giving advice and support, fellow club members can be the source of livestock, including coral frags and live sand critters. They will also be able to direct you to the most reliable retailers in your area. Club members often pool orders for equipment or livestock to take advantage of bulk pricing.

## Going Berlin

The Berlin system was mentioned in Chapter 3. In this system, the tank is well stocked with live rock, and an efficient protein skimmer is used. In the popular modified version, live sand is added for increased nitrate reduction. One or more powerheads might be employed to create significant currents, especially if reef invertebrates are going to be included in the tank.

To convert your aquarium, you might need to add live rock, and you would remove the power filters. This is not a step to be taken lightly, as those

SMALL FRY

### Future Hobbyists

It is possible that a child raised in a home with a marine aquarium will keep his or her excitement and become a lifelong aquarist. Encouraging a younger child to participate in the maintenance and enjoyment of the aquarium will provide a hands-on learning experience far more productive than any video game.

filters have been compensating for a variety of possible shortcomings in the system and in your fledgling husbandry skills. It is especially vital that your aquarium be understocked for a Berlin setup to work. Still, if you remove one filter and wait a few weeks before removing the other, you will have time to adjust your aquarium husbandry to keep water conditions optimal.

## A Reef Aquarium

Maintaining a fish-only-with-live-rock Berlin system is excellent practice for moving on to a reef aquarium, but your first reef tank should be larger than the one in our protocol here—at least 75 to 100 gallons (300 to 400 liters). A reef aquarium is outside our protocol, but there are many good books on starting a reef tank that you can

Starting a reef aquarium is outside the protocol of this book, but others are available for your perusal on this subject.

consult when you are ready to take that step.

## Captive Breeding

In most cases, the breakthroughs in captive breeding of marine animals have been made by hobbyists. If you are interested in this important aspect of the hobby, read everything and talk to as many people as you can so that you can decide for sure whether this is a direction you want to follow, and if so, how best to go about it.

The problem around which everything else revolves is that almost all marines have a planktonic larval stage. Plankton have little power of locomotion and just drift with the currents. Even when the eggs are guarded by a parent, the fry are minuscule and float up into the plankton raft, where they feed on even smaller organisms. After a period of time, the larvae metamorphose and settle out—they transform into miniature fish and take their places in the reef.

It is that larval period that causes the problems. The shape of the vessel, the lighting, and the water conditions are all designed to overcome these problems, and the culturing of planktonic food organisms usually requires more space, time, and effort than the rearing of the fry. Nevertheless, the reward can be great. This is a great time to be involved in breeding marine ornamentals—enough pioneering groundwork has been done to get you started, but many of the secrets remain to be discovered.

Whatever course you take, the protocol in this book will have given you a solid start in the marine aquarium hobby, and your aquarium will be a piece of natural beauty you and your family and friends can enjoy.

# Resources

## Magazines

**Tropical Fish Hobbyist**
1 TFH Plaza
3rd & Union Avenues
Neptune City, NJ 07753
E-mail: info@tfh.com
www.tfhmagazine.com

## Internet Resources

**Aquaria Central**
www.aquariacentral.com

**Aquarium Hobbyist**
www.aquariumhobbyist.com

**A World of Fish**
www.aworldoffish.com

**Fish Geeks**
www.fishgeeks.com

**Marine Aquarium Advice**
www.marineaquariumadvice.com

**Reef Central**
www.reefcentral.com

**Tropical Resources**
www.tropicalresources.net

**Wet Web Media**
www.wetwebmedia.com

## Associations & Societies

**Federation of American Aquarium Societies (FAAS)**
E-mail: Jbenes01@yahoo.com
www.faas.info

**Federation of British Aquatic Societies (FBAS)**
E-mail: webmaster@fbas.co.uk
www.fbas.co.uk

**Marine Aquarium Council (MAC)**
E-mail: info@aquariumcouncil.org
www.aquariumcouncil.org

**Marine Aquarium Societies of North America (MASNA)**
E-mail: secretary@masna.org
www.masna.org

**National Aquarium in Baltimore**
501 E. Pratt Street
Baltimore, MD 21202
(410) 576-3800
www.aqua.org

## Books

Boruchowitz, David E., *The Guide to Starting a Marine Aquarium*, TFH Publications.

Boruchowitz, David E., *Saltwater Aquarium Setup & Care*, TFH Publications.

Saltwater Aquariums

Fenner, Robert M., *The Conscientious Marine Aquarist*, TFH Publications.

Kurtz, Jeffrey, *The Super Simple Guide to Marine Aquariums*, TFH Publications.

Michael, Scott W., *A PocketExpert™ Guide to Marine Fishes*, TFH Publications.

Michael, Scott W., *Reef Fishes Volume 1*, TFH Publications.

Michael, Scott W., *Reef Fishes Volume 2: Basslets, Dottybacks & Hawkfishes*, TFH Publications.

Michael, Scott W., *Reef Fishes Volume 3: Angelfishes & Butterflyfishes*, TFH Publications.

Skomal, Gregory, *Clownfishes in the Aquarium*, TFH Publications.

Resources

# Index

Note: **Boldfaced** numbers indicate illustrations; an italic *t* indicates tables.

Saltwater Aquariums

111

Index

## Dedication

This book is dedicated to my grandchildren, who keep me young and remind me what life is really about.

## About the Author

David E. Boruchowitz is in his sixth decade of fishkeeping. He has been writing and editing for TFH Publications for more than 10 years and has authored a large number of books on a variety of topics. He currently serves as Editor-in-Chief of *Tropical Fish Hobbyist* Magazine. One of his priorities is making the aquarium hobby accessible to everyone, and many of his projects involve simplifying aquarium husbandry so beginners can succeed on their first attempt.

## Photo Credits

Gerald R. Allen, 90
Lawrence Azoulay, 91
CR Brightwell, 4, 16
James Fatherree, 88
Rob Fenner, 70
Bill Gately, 66
G.W. Lange, 23
Stuart Levine, 31
Marotta Michele, 49
MP. & C. Piednoir, 100
Pieter, 25

Courtney Platt, 80 (bottom)
J. Randall, 80 (top)
G. Schmelzer, 38
Chen Wei Seng, 51
Mark Smith, 18, 21, 36, 45, 54, 75, 76 (top)
Iggy Tavares, 67, 69, 78, 82, 87
Edward Taylor, 77

All other photos courtesy of T.F.H. photo archives

**REACH OUT. ACT. RESPOND.**
Go to AnimalPlanet.com/ROAR and find out how you can be a voice for animals everywhere!

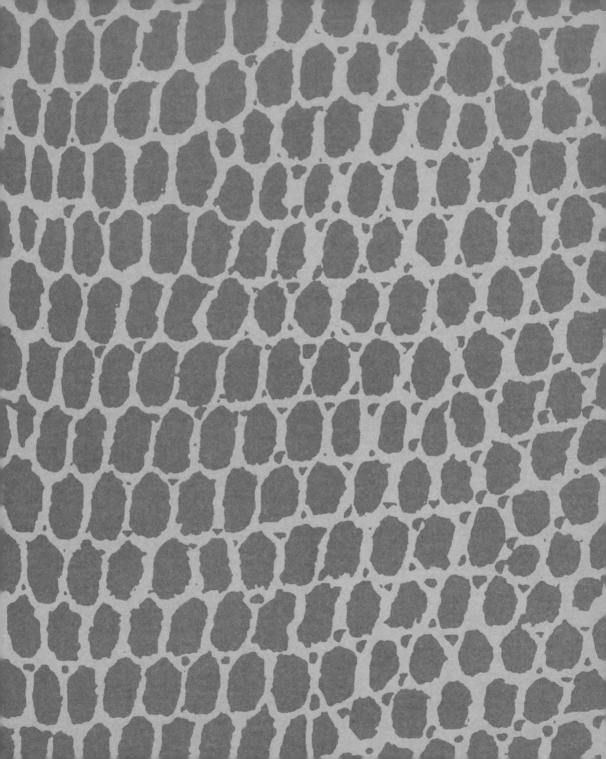